FRYDERYK CHOPIN

WALTZES

for Piano / für Klavier

Edited by / Herausgegeben von
Christophe Grabowski

Series Editors:

John Rink, Jim Samson, Jean-Jacques Eigeldinger & Christophe Grabowski

ALLE RECHTE VORBEHALTEN · ALL RIGHTS RESERVED

EDITION PETERS
LEIPZIG · LONDON · NEW YORK

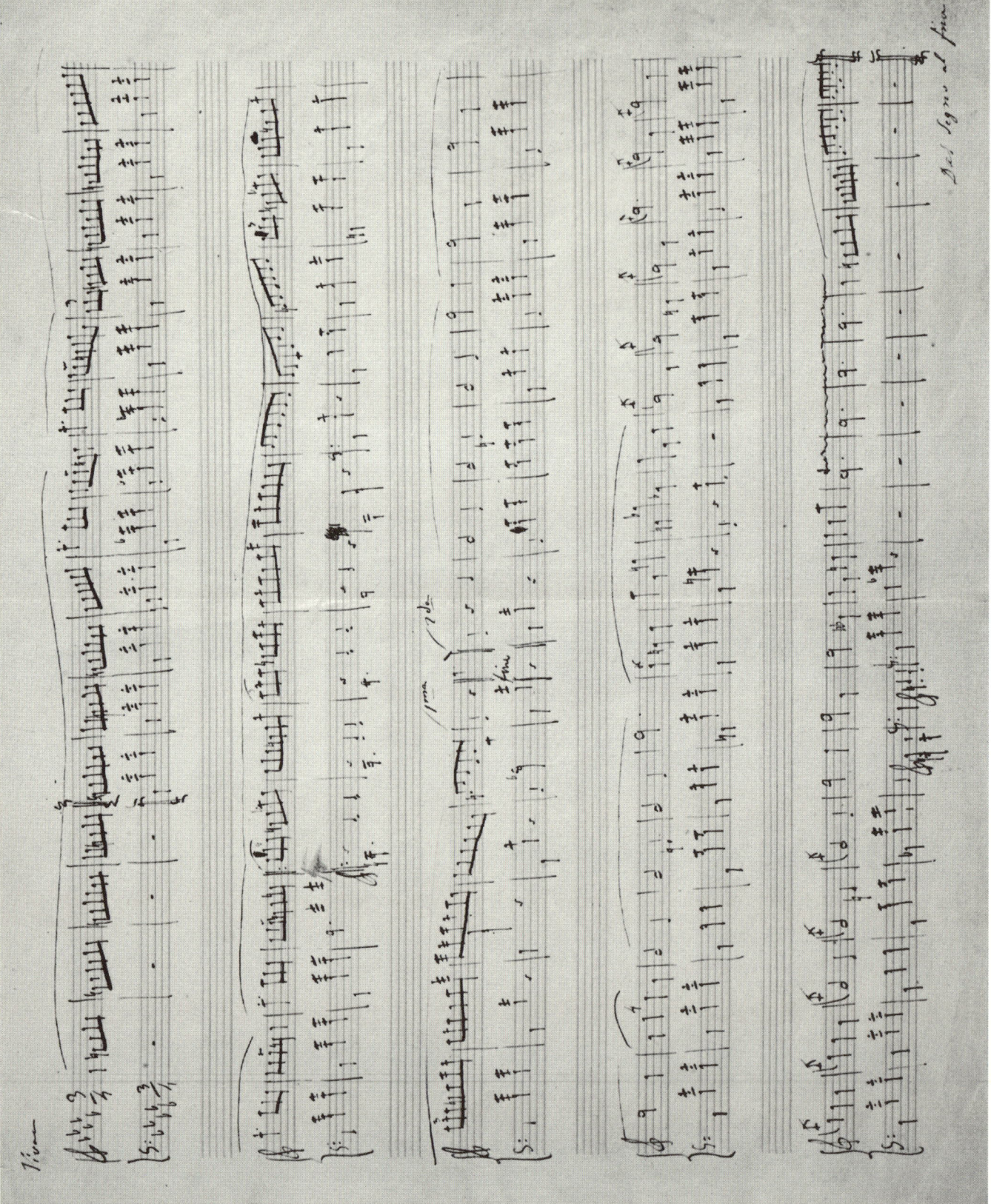

Walrz Op. 64 No. 1, autograph presented to Juliette de Caraman (**A⁵**). London, Royal College of Music.

Valse op. 64 n° 1, autographe offert à Juliette de Caraman (**A⁵**). London, Royal College of Music.

Walzer op. 64 Nr. 1, Autograph überreicht an Juliette de Caraman (**A⁵**). London, Royal College of Music.

CONTENTS

Preface v
Préface vii
Vorwort ix

WALTZ OP. 18
Page No.

1

WALTZ OP. 34 NO. 1

10

WALTZ OP. 34 NO. 2

20

WALTZ OP. 34 NO. 3

26

WALTZ OP. 42

30

WALTZ OP. 64 NO. 1
Page No.

40

WALTZ OP. 64 NO. 2

44

WALTZ OP. 64 NO. 3

50

WALTZ in B minor (composed 1829)
Version based on C¹ (see source information, p. 134)
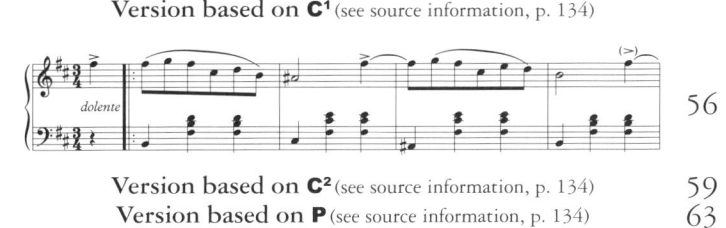
56

Version based on **C²** (see source information, p. 134) 59
Version based on **P** (see source information, p. 134) 63

WALTZ in D♭ major (composed 1829)

66

WALTZ in E major (composed 1829/30)

Page No. 69

WALTZ in A♭ major (composed 1830)
Version based on **A** (see source information, p. 135)

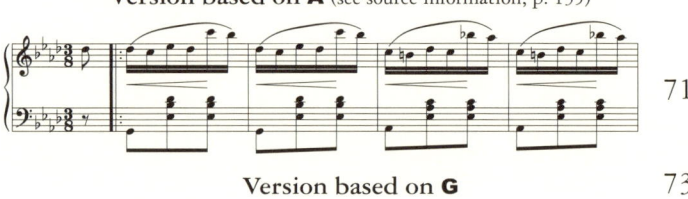
71

Version based on **G** 73
(see source information, p. 135)

WALTZ in E minor (composed 1830)

75

WALTZ in G♭ major (composed 1832)
Version based on **A¹** (see source information, p. 136)

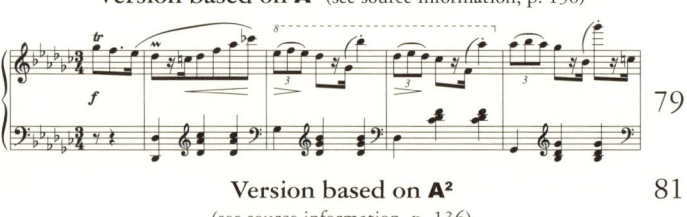
79

Version based on **A²** 81
(see source information, p. 136)

WALTZ in A♭ major (composed 1835)
Version based on **A¹** (see source information, p. 136)

Page No. 83

Version based on **A³** with variants 85
(see source information, p. 136–137)

WALTZ in F minor (composed 1842)
Version based on **A³** (see source information, p. 137)

88

Version based on **A⁵** with variants 90
(see source information, p. 137–138)

Version based on **P** 92
(see source information, p. 138)

WALTZ in A minor (composed 1847)

94

APPENDIX

WALTZ OP. 18 (version based on **A¹**) 96
(see source information, p. 125)

WALTZ OP. 18 (version based on **A²**) 101
(see source information, p. 125)

WALTZ OP. 34 NO. 1 (version based on **A¹**) 108
(see source information, p. 126)

WALTZ OP. 64 NO. 1 115
(version based on **A³** with variants)
(see source information, p. 131)

WALTZ OP. 64 NO. 2 (version based on **A²**) 118
(see source information, p. 132)

NOTES ON EDITORIAL METHOD AND PRACTICE..................123
CRITICAL COMMENTARY..................125

PREFACE*

Chopin and the waltz

There is evidence to suggest that waltzes featured among Chopin's very first and last compositions alike. He inscribed his earliest waltzes in the album of Countess Izabella Grabowska some time before 1825. That album no longer survives, however, nor do seven waltzes composed between 1826 and 1830 which are known only from the incipits prepared by Chopin's sister Ludwika Jędrzejewicz shortly after the composer's death in 1849. As for his final waltz, which Chopin presented to Katherine Erskine in October 1848, only a reproduction of its title page still exists.

Chopin's lifelong predilection for dance forms is widely recognised, and he would have been especially familiar with the waltz from an early age. Like other European capitals, Warsaw succumbed to the charms of the waltz from 1810 onward, to the extent that more traditional dances were altogether supplanted apart from the mazur and the polonaise. According to Wojciech Tomaszewski, the first waltz to be published in Poland appeared in 1815, the year of the final Congress of Vienna, which conferred noble status upon a once humble dance form. Thereafter every Polish composer – with the exception of Chopin's serious-minded teacher, Józef Elsner – began to write waltzes, their main function remaining purely utilitarian. In short, these waltzes were meant to be danced to, whether at public balls or at the *soirées dansantes* held in private, sometimes domestic settings. It is there that the young Fryderyk heard his first waltzes, and the incipits mentioned above reveal an unpretentious musical style eminently suited to dancing.

Chopin's two visits to Vienna in 1829 and 1831 seem to have changed his attitude to the waltz. Nevertheless, his unwillingness to accord artistic status to the genre is confirmed by an ironic comment in his letter to Elsner of 29 January 1831, in which he writes that 'waltzes are regarded as works here! and Strauss and Lanner, who play them for dancing to, are hailed as "*Kapellmeisters*"!'. That did not prevent him from writing a waltz of his own while in Vienna, however, though its existence is known only from a reference in a letter to his family of 22 December 1830. Chopin's letter also contains a significant remark about some of his early mazurkas, which he takes pains to point out were not 'meant for dancing'. Not until he settled in Paris would he think of the waltz in similar terms.

Five waltzes date from the end of the Warsaw period. The A♭ major – the only waltz by Chopin in $\frac{3}{8}$ – has a lively, whirling character which alludes to the utilitarian function of the dance but also to more folk-inspired influences. By contrast, the waltzes in E major, B minor, D♭ major and E minor bear Chopin's personal stamp, the genre's lyrical aspect increasingly being brought to the fore. In the case of the D♭ Waltz, the adolescent Chopin unusually revealed his source of inspiration: the young singer Konstancja Gładkowska, his 'ideal'. When sending the autograph score to his friend and confidant Tytus Woyciechowski, Chopin drew the latter's attention to a bar marked with a cross, the point where the work's emotional expression reached its peak.

Only eight of the twelve waltzes composed after Chopin's establishment in Paris were published during his lifetime. Comparison of the different versions of Op. 18, Op. 34 No. 1, Op. 64 No.1 and Op. 64 No. 2 clearly reveals his efforts to perfect them. A letter from Auguste Franchomme to Jules Forest reveals the exact moment when Chopin added the coda to the Waltz Op. 18 – namely, the very day on which he completed the copy intended for the publisher (i.e. *Stichvorlage*). The means by which Op. 34 No. 1 reached its final form was similar, the code once again making its first appearance in the definitive version of the score. Close examination of the *Stichvorlage* for Op. 64 No. 1 indicates that the final cascade was likewise added at a very late stage – a stage of enhancement from which the waltzes held back from publication (Nos. 15–18) did not benefit, all four being cast in an identical *da capo* mould. This group of works belongs to a category of intimate pieces of generally melancholic character. The sole exception is the earliest, in G♭ major, in which the prevailing mood is one of carefree joy laced with tenderness. Chopin presented these waltzes to friends and pupils as a tribute and did not want them to be made more widely available, a point emphasised in a letter to Caroline de Belleville-Oury, to whom one of several manuscripts of the F minor Waltz was presented.

Not a single waltz was styled by Chopin himself as 'grand', 'brilliant' or 'melancholic' – epithets added instead by his publishers and in some cases radically in opposition to their underlying character. Nowhere is the contrast starker and more absurd than in the case of the A minor Waltz Op. 34 No. 2, which, like the other two in the opus, was marketed by Maurice Schlesinger as a *Grande Valse brillante*. Another publisher notorious for inventing fanciful titles – Christian Rudolph Wessel – dubbed Op. 18 'Invitation pour la danse' in a direct reference to Carl Maria von Weber's famous *Aufforderung zum Tanz* Op. 65.

Robert Schumann was one of the first to appreciate the true worth of Chopin's waltzes, which he recognised as outstanding examples of the genre and as projecting the unmistakable originality of all the composer's works. For Schumann, the A♭ Waltz Op. 42 was thoroughly aristocratic in character, a point he underscored by attributing to the fictional Florestan (one of his literary alter egos) the comment that if this waltz were played at a ball, at least half the ladies dancing 'would have to be countesses'.

The waltz before and after Chopin

The middle of the nineteenth century marked the golden age of the waltz, which had progressed spectacularly from its distant folk origins to the aristocratic salon. The oldest waltzes comprise two eight-bar periods, while the next evolutionary stage introduced an extension of these two halves for the sake of greater contrast. The opening section was then repeated, producing a da capo form with a central Trio, a type well represented in Chopin's output. An even more developed form can be found in Weber's *Aufforderung zum Tanz*, which consists of a suite of waltzes preceded by an introduction and ending with a coda, a model adopted by Chopin in many of his Paris waltzes.

Innumerable composers were drawn to the waltz, not least the *Tanzcomponisten* (composers of dance music) who churned out waltzes for the piano by the yard. Most of these are now unknown outside the libraries that hold their yellowing scores. Those of Schubert and Beethoven – which exemplify the first two stages in the waltz's evolution – have survived thanks to their composers' reputations, though it is worth remembering that one of Beethoven's most fascinating compositions, his Thirty-Three Variations Op. 120, is based on a thoroughly banal waltz theme by Anton Diabelli. Among Chopin's contemporaries, only Liszt took the waltz genre into really new territory, raising virtuosity to heights that have never been reached again, notably in his *Mephisto Waltz*. A generation later, Brahms brought an expressive nobility to his Waltzes Op. 39 – a set of sixteen waltzes originally scored for piano four hands and transcribed by the composer himself for piano solo. Fauré's *Valses-Caprices* fail to match the level of inspiration achieved by his nocturnes and barcarolles, whereas scattered flashes of genius colour Saint-Saëns's *Étude en forme de Valse*. Debussy's *La plus que lente*, immortalised by its composer in the form of a piano roll, is more a parody of French sentimentality than a homage to a genre which by the beginning of the twentieth century was already in decline. And yet the essential qualities of the waltz were again to find magisterial expression in Ravel's *Valses nobles et sentimentales*, one of the last examples of a piano waltz and a veritable jewel of the keyboard repertory.

---

* I should like to thank Jean-Jacques Eigeldinger and John Rink for their invaluable comments on this introduction.

As for orchestral music, pride of place must go to Johann Strauss and his three sons, whose immortal waltzes conjure up a musical panorama of Viennese life. But the waltz also occurs in symphonic works by Berlioz, Tchaikovsky, Mahler and Shostakovich, and in the operas of Gounod, Tchaikovsky, Offenbach, Massenet, Leoncavallo, Puccini, Richard Strauss and Berg, and even in Wagner's *Parsifal*. Ubiquitous in operettas, waltzes are hardly less prevalent in nineteenth- and early twentieth-century ballets. Ravel was one of the last composers to pay tribute to the waltz in his dazzling 'choreographic poem' *La Valse* (1919–20), which can be seen as the apotheosis of the genre.

Performing Chopin's waltzes

According to various eyewitness accounts, Chopin improvised mazurkas and other dances – including waltzes – at private *soirées* in Warsaw and Paris. He performed some of his finished waltzes at his last concert in Paris in 1848 and also during his public appearances in England and Scotland later that year.

Wilhelm von Lenz's 'Critical Survey of Chopin's Piano Compositions'[1] reports that Chopin played the A♭ Waltz Op. 42 'in a *prestissimo* movement with continuous *stretto* while maintaining a steady beat in the bass', and that in his view the work should be rendered 'like musical clockwork'. Lenz relates furthermore that in the D♭ Waltz Op. 64 No. 1 Chopin 'reduced the length of the first four bars almost by half',[2] whereas the composer himself explained that 'it should unroll like a ball of string', the real tempo beginning only with the bass in bar 5. According to Lenz, Chopin was almost impossible to please in the C-sharp minor Waltz Op. 64 No. 2: 'He alone knew the right way to tie the *single* semiquaver to the following crotchet in bars 3–4!'

Equally noteworthy is Joseph Schiffmacher's advice, presumably derived from the composer himself, that the third beat in the left-hand accompaniment should be played in a lighter, more subtle manner throughout the C-sharp minor Waltz, likewise his suggestion that the right-hand sixth in bar 2 of the same piece should be arpeggiated.[3]

As for the performance of works reproduced here in multiple versions and also those for which a single composite version has been proposed, the performer is strongly encouraged to adhere to a single source as far as possible. The variants unique to each one form an integrated whole whose internal logic may reveal itself only after prolonged contact. Combining elements from the different versions is to be recommended only to experienced performers with a sophisticated and ramified understanding of Chopin's creative process.

---

[1] Wilhelm von Lenz, 'Uebersichtliche Beurtheilung der Pianoforte-Compositionen von Chopin, als Prodromus eines kritischen Katalogs seiner sämmtlichen Werke', *Neue Berliner Musikzeitung*, 26 (1872), pp. 282–3, 289–92, 297–9. Details of French and English translations of Lenz's survey are provided in the Bibliography.

[2] This testimony must be treated with caution as Lenz did not see Chopin again after his few lessons in 1842. It is likely that Lenz misinterpreted comments made to him by one or another of Chopin's pupils. Nevertheless, when playing the D♭ Waltz, Chopin may have treated the tempo of the introduction flexibly, gradually growing faster – hence the metaphor of a ball of string unrolling.

[3] For further information about this late pupil of Chopin's, see Aline Tasset, *La main et l'âme au piano d'après Schiffmacher* (Paris: Delagrave, 1908), and Jean-Jacques Eigeldinger, *Chopin vu par ses élèves* (Neuchâtel: La Baconnière, 1988), pp. 132–3, 234; trans. Naomi Shohet with Krysia Osostowicz and Roy Howat as *Chopin: Pianist and Teacher as Seen by His Pupils*, ed. Roy Howat (Cambridge: Cambridge University Press, 1986), pp. 88, 179. The 'tradition' of arpeggiating the sixth in Op. 64 No. 2, imprecisely described by Tasset (the F double-sharp cannot be executed in the same way as the anacrusis, i.e. on the third beat), has been questioned by Jean-Jacques Eigeldinger and may originally have pertained to Op. 34 No. 1, in which the sixths are also arpeggiated (see bars 17, 18, 20–22, 25, 26, 29, 30 *et seq.* in the version based on **A¹**).

Structure of volume

The eight waltzes with authentic opus numbers appear in the order in which they were published, followed by those released after 1849. Dating from Chopin's Warsaw and Paris periods alike, the posthumously published waltzes – over half the works in this volume – are arranged in order of composition.[4] Excluded from this edition are two works of doubtful authenticity which feature in Chomiński and Turło's *Katalog* (respectively pp. 246 and 250): the Waltz in A♭ major and, of even more uncertain provenance, the Waltz in F♯ minor.

The Critical Commentary indicates the existence of an exceptional amount of source material for many of the waltzes in this volume. In editing the posthumously published works, priority has been given to Chopin's autograph scores rather than the versions published by Julian Fontana, the latter having served as the main reference source for virtually every critical edition released since 1855. With the sole exception of the Waltz in D♭ major, for which no manuscript has survived, Fontana's edition has been treated here as a secondary rather than primary source, principally yielding a number of variants which may be authentic though they appear in no other source.

Another distinctive feature of the present edition lies in the way in which it uses the available sources for given works. These sources often include several autograph manuscripts reflecting distinct stages in the genesis of the works in question, thus meriting far greater significance than that accorded in most modern editions. Contrary to the view of many an editor, these multiple autographs are not of mere musicological interest, since they offer invaluable insights to performers seeking an interpretation that respects the composer's intentions. In allowing us to trace the work's evolution in all its fascinating detail, the sources also reveal the human side of Chopin's unceasing quest for perfection – that is, for the most precisely notated form of his musical thoughts. The legacy of this creative effort is rich in instruction for those who choose to observe it.

The sheer number of surviving versions has required judicious selection and certain organisational decisions in preparing this new edition:

- In the case of Op. 18, Op. 34 No. 1, and Op. 64 Nos. 1 and 2, the versions predating those submitted to the publishers are included in the Appendix – a distinction that seems to be warranted for various reasons. As for Op. 64 No. 1, the variants deriving from all three surviving autograph manuscripts have been collated in a composite version in order to facilitate comparison of the different sources.
- The different versions of the waltzes released after 1849 appear in sequence within the main body of the volume. Since Chopin's own preferences remain unclear, these versions must be regarded as having equivalent status. Therefore performers are free to choose whichever version suits them best. In the case of the A♭ major and F minor Waltzes, for which numerous sources survive, the editorial process has been similar to that described for Op. 64 No. 1. A third version of the Waltzes in B minor and F minor is provided, reflecting the text of the first Polish edition (1852); the latter was based on a manuscript which has since been lost.

Some of these versions are familiar from the publications of Édouard Ganche (1930), Alicja Simon (1949), Heinrich Neuhaus and Yakov Milstein (1953), and Byron Janis (1978); a number also appear in many available Urtexts. The version of the A♭ Waltz Op. 34 No. 1 based on the autograph manuscript within the album of the Thun-Hohenstein sisters has been prepared from poor reproductions which

---

[4] This system of classification avoids the opus numbers 66–74 assigned not by Julian Fontana (an incorrect attribution found throughout the literature) but by Adolphe-Martin Schlesinger, the German publisher of Chopin's posthumous works. Some composition dates are subject to controversy; those given here are taken from Chomiński and Turło's *Katalog* (see Bibliography).

are extremely difficult to decipher. The album itself was lost in the turmoil of the Second World War, and until such time as it resurfaces, no edition of this version of the Waltz can be regarded as definitive, including the one offered here.

Bibliography

EIGELDINGER, JEAN-JACQUES, *Chopin vu par ses élèves* (Neuchâtel: La Baconnière, 1988); trans. Naomi Shohet with Krysia Osostowicz and Roy Howat as *Chopin: Pianist and Teacher as Seen by His Pupils*, ed. Roy Howat (Cambridge: Cambridge University Press, 1986)

GRABOWSKI, CHRISTOPHE & RINK, JOHN, *Annotated Catalogue of Chopin's First Editions* (Cambridge: CUP, 2010)

GUIGNARD, SILVAIN, *Frédéric Chopins Walzer: Eine text- und stilkritische Studie* (Baden-Baden: Koerner, 1986)

KOBYLAŃSKA, KRYSTYNA, *Rękopisy utworów Chopina – Katalog* (Kraków: PWM, 1977)

LENZ, WILHELM von, *Die großen Pianoforte-Virtuosen unserer Zeit aus persönlicher Bekanntschaft: Liszt – Chopin – Tausig – Henselt* (Berlin: Behr, 1972); trans. Jean-Jacques Eigeldinger as *Les grands virtuoses du piano: Liszt, Chopin, Tausig, Henselt* (Paris: Flammarion, 1995); trans. Madeleine R. Baker as *The Great Piano Virtuosos of Our Time from Personal Acquaintance: Liszt, Chopin, Tausig, Henselt* (New York: G. Schirmer, 1899; R1971 and 1983)

RUHLMANN, SOPHIE, 'Chopin – Franchomme', in *Chopin w kręgu przyjaciół*, vol. 2 (Warsaw: Neriton, 1996)

SCHUMANN, ROBERT, *Gesammelte Schriften über Musik und Musiker* (Leipzig: Breitkopf & Härtel, 1891); partially trans. Henry Pleasants as *The Musical World of Robert Schumann* (London: Victor Gollancz Ltd, 1965)

TOMASZEWSKI, WOJCIECH, *Bibliografia warszawskich druków muzycznych 1801–1850* (Warsaw: Biblioteka Narodowa, 1992)

Christophe Grabowski
Translated by Stewart Spencer and John Rink

PRÉFACE*

Chopin et la Valse

Si les informations dont nous disposons sont exactes, les valses feraient partie aussi bien des premières que des dernières œuvres de Chopin. Celles d'avant 1825, contenues dans l'album de la comtesse Izabella Grabowska, semblent définitivement perdues. Sept autres, composées entre 1826 et 1830, ne sont connues que par des incipit confectionnés par Ludwika Jędrzejewicz peu après la mort de son frère. De la dernière valse – offerte par le compositeur à Katherine Erskine en octobre 1848 – seule la reproduction de la page de titre est actuellement accessible.

Outre la prédilection que Chopin montre pour les formes dansantes, la valse est sans doute l'une de celles qui lui ont été plus particulièrement familières dès son enfance. Il est à rappeler que dans les années 1810, Varsovie, comme d'autres capitales européennes, succombe au charme de la valse qui, peu à peu, y supplante les danses traditionnelles ; seuls le *mazur* et la *polonaise* lui résistent. D'après la bibliographie de Wojciech Tomaszewski, la première valse imprimée dans la patrie de Chopin le fut en 1815 (l'année de clôture du Congrès de Vienne – événement qui apporta à cette danse ses titres de noblesse). A partir de cette date, tous les compositeurs polonais, exception faite du très sérieux Józef Elsner, se sont mis à écrire au rythme de la valse dont le rôle premier – purement utilitaire – était de faire danser : aux bals ou au cours de soirées dansantes données dans un cadre privé, voire familial. Ainsi l'entendra également le jeune Frédéric. Les incipit évoqués ci-dessus manifestent une musique sans prétention, destinée tout simplement à danser.

Les deux séjours à Vienne modifieront son regard sur cette danse. Cependant, comme le montre l'ironie de cette citation extraite de la lettre du 29 janvier 1831 à Elsner « ici les valses sont considérées comme des œuvres et on appelle 'chefs d'orchestre' Strauss et Lanner qui les jouent pour faire danser ! », Chopin ne lui accorde toujours pas de statut artistique ; ce qui ne l'empêche pas, pour autant, d'en composer une, précisément dans cette ville. Il annonce la création de cette valse, qui nous est inconnue, dans la lettre du 22 décembre 1830 à sa famille, où l'on relève une remarque significative concernant les mazurkas : celles qu'il vient d'écrire ne sont plus « faites pour être dansées ». Le même changement d'optique s'opérera pour les valses, plus tard, seulement à Paris.

Cinq valses datent de la période d'entre 1829 et 1830. Celle en La bémol majeur (l'unique à être notée à $\frac{3}{8}$) – virevoltante et pleine d'entrain, évoquant par son caractère les danses populaires – est encore profondément ancrée dans la fonction utilitaire. En revanche, les valses en Mi majeur, en Si mineur, en Ré bémol majeur et en Mi mineur sont déjà empreintes d'un cachet plus personnel ; le côté lyrique commence à y être davantage mis en valeur. Pour l'une d'entre elles, fait très rare, le jeune adolescent dévoile sa source d'inspiration : l'idéal personnifié par la jeune cantatrice Konstancja Gładkowska. Dans la lettre qui accompagne le manuscrit de la valse en Ré bémol, il attire l'attention de son ami et confident Tytus Woyciechowski sur une mesure marquée d'une croix – endroit où l'effusion des sentiments devrait atteindre son sommet.

Seules huit des douze valses composées après l'installation de Chopin à Paris ont été publiées par lui. La comparaison entre les différentes versions des opus 18, 34 n° 1, 64 n°^{os} 1 & 2, donne une image précise du progrès accompli dans leur perfectionnement. Un passage de la correspondance d'Auguste Franchomme à Jules Forest, nous renseigne sur le moment exact du rajout de la coda dans l'opus 18, effectué seulement le jour de l'achèvement du manuscrit éditorial. Le processus de maturation de la seconde composition citée a été très semblable, puisque la coda n'apparaît que dans sa version définitive. Un regard attentif sur le manuscrit éditorial de la Valse op. 64 n° 1 suffit pour constater l'addition très tardive du trait final en gamme – genre d'améliorations qui ne sera jamais introduit dans les quatre valses non retenues pour la publication (n°^{os} 15–18), épousant toutes une immuable forme *da capo*. Ces dernières appartiennent à une catégorie d'œuvres intimes de caractère mélancolique, à l'exception de la plus ancienne d'entre elles (en Sol bémol majeur) où la joyeuse insouciance agrémentée d'une pointe de douceur règne encore sans partage. Le compositeur les offrait en hommage à des amis et élèves, et ne souhaitait pas leur divulgation. Il le précisa clairement dans une lettre à Caroline de Belleville-Oury – une des destinataires du manuscrit de la valse en Fa mineur.

Chopin n'a qualifié aucune de ses valses de *grande*, de *brillante* ou de *mélancolique* ; ces adjectifs viennent des éditeurs et tels d'entre eux sont même en opposition totale avec le caractère de l'opus 34 n° 2 qui, comme les deux autres pièces du même opus, a été baptisée *Grande Valse brillante* par Maurice Schlesinger. Christian Rudolph Wessel – connu pour son habitude d'inventer des titres fantaisistes – a nommé l'opus 18 *Invitation pour la danse* – en souvenir de la célèbre *Aufforderung zum Tanz* op. 65 de Carl Maria von Weber.

---

* Je tiens à exprimer mes plus vifs remerciements à Jean-Jacques Eigeldinger et à John Rink pour leurs précieuses remarques concernant ce texte.

En reconnaissant que les valses de Chopin incarnent ce qu'il y a de meilleur dans le genre, et, aussi, en soulignant qu'elles sont empreintes, comme toutes ses œuvres, d'un cachet inimitable, Robert Schumann fut parmi les premiers à les apprécier à leur juste valeur. Pour lui, l'expression de l'opus 42 est éminemment aristocratique, et, pour appuyer ce propos, il fait dire à Florestan – un de ses *alter ego* littéraires – que s'il l'on exécutait cette valse au cour d'un bal, « il faudrait que la bonne moitié des danseuses fussent pour le moins comtesses ».

La valse avant et après Chopin

Le milieu du XIXe siècle marque l'apogée de cette danse aux origines beaucoup plus lointaines. Sans remonter à ses sources, certainement populaires, ni retracer sa spectaculaire ascension sociale de la fête paysanne au salon aristocratique, il convient d'indiquer que les plus anciennes des valses étaient composées de deux périodes de huit mesures chacune. L'échelon suivant de l'évolution a consisté à allonger les deux parties, à contraster davantage leur caractère, puis, à introduire une reprise, aboutissant ainsi sur une coupe *da capo* avec *trio* – bien représentée chez Chopin. Le modèle encore plus développé de la forme se cristallise dans l'*Aufforderung zum Tanz* de Weber constituée d'une suite de valses précédées d'une introduction et s'achevant par une coda – référence utilisée par Chopin dans bon nombre de ses valses parisiennes.

La liste des compositeurs attirés par cette danse est des plus longues. Dans le domaine du piano, les *faiseurs de danses (Tanzcomponisten)* sont légion ; leurs créations, autrefois célèbres, encombrent aujourd'hui les rayons des bibliothèques. Celles de Schubert et de Beethoven, illustrant les deux premières étapes de l'évolution, survivent grâce à la notoriété de leurs auteurs. Il est toutefois à rappeler que l'une des compositions les plus fascinantes du maître de Bonn – les *33 Variations* op. 120 – prend pour thème une insignifiante valse de Diabelli. Parmi les contemporains de Chopin, seul Franz Liszt a su ouvrir de nouveaux horizons à cette danse, en élevant la virtuosité à un niveau jusqu'à aujourd'hui inégalé dans sa diabolique *Méphisto Valse*. Compositeur de la génération suivante, Johannes Brahms, animé d'une noble expression son œuvre 39 – suite de valses à 4 mains transcrite également pour piano seul par l'auteur lui-même. Les *Valses-Caprices* de Gabriel Fauré n'atteignent pas la hauteur de ses nocturnes ou barcarolles. Quelques éclats épars de génie apparaissent dans l'*Etude en forme de Valse* de Camille Saint-Saëns. *La plus que lente* de Claude Debussy, immortalisée par son créateur dans un enregistrement sur rouleaux, est davantage un pastiche de la sentimentalité française qu'un hommage au genre déjà en plein déclin au début du XXe siècle. Les qualités essentielles de cette danse s'expriment magistralement dans l'un des derniers joyaux de la littérature pianistique qui lui a été consacré : *Valses nobles et sentimentales* de Maurice Ravel.

En ce qui concerne le répertoire pour orchestre, Johann Strauss et ses trois fils avec leurs immortelles valses qui dépeignent en musique toutes les scènes de la vie viennoise sont à citer en premier lieu. Cette danse apparaît également dans la musique symphonique de Berlioz, Tchaïkovski, Mahler et Chostakovitch, dans les opéras de Gounod, Tchaïkovski, Offenbach, Massenet, Leoncavallo, Puccini, R. Strauss, Berg et même chez Wagner (*Parsifal*). Elle est très présente dans d'innombrables opérettes et pratiquement dans tous les ballets du XIXe et du début du XXe siècle. Maurice Ravel fut l'un des derniers à lui rendre un éclatant hommage dans le poème chorégraphique intitulé *La Valse* (1920) où cette danse atteint son apothéose.

Interprétation des Valses

Il existe des témoignages sur Chopin improvisant des mazurkas et d'autres danses (très certainement des valses) au cours de soirées privées à Varsovie et à Paris. Ses valses figuraient au programme de son dernier concert parisien ; il les a également fait entendre lors de ses prestations publiques en Angleterre et en Ecosse, en 1848.

Dans son *Panorama de l'oeuvre de Chopin en vue d'un catalogue critique*[1], Wilhelm von Lenz rapporte que Chopin jouait la Valse op. 42 « dans un mouvement *prestissimo* de strette continue en maintenant ferme la mesure dans les basses » et que, selon ses termes, l'oeuvre en question devrait être rendue « dans l'esprit d'une boîte à musique ». Il relate aussi que dans la première valse de l'opus 64 Chopin « réduisait approximativement à deux la durée des quatre mesures initiales »[2] qui, d'après le compositeur, « sont à dévider comme une pelote ». Le mouvement était seulement donné par la basse dans la cinquième mesure. De même, Lenz affirme que dans la deuxième pièce du même opus, on avait du mal à satisfaire Chopin qui « lui seul s'y entendait pour lier convenablement l'unique double croche à la noire qui suit dans les mesures 3–4 ! ».

Le conseil transmis par Joseph Schiffmacher, venant vraisemblablement du compositeur et concernant l'exécution – nuancée et plus légère – de tous les troisièmes temps de l'accompagnement de la main gauche, ainsi que la suggestion d'arpéger la sixte de la main droite à la seconde mesure de l'opus 64 no 2, sont aussi à retenir[3].

Pour ce qui est de l'interprétation des œuvres reproduites en versions multiples et de celles pour lesquelles nous proposons une version de synthèse, l'éditeur du volume recommande vivement de suivre autant que possible une seule source. Les variantes propres à chacune d'elles présentent un ensemble d'une logique supérieure qui échappe souvent à la première lecture. L'amalgame entre les versions n'est conseillé qu'aux interprètes avertis et bien renseignés sur les particularités du processus de création chez Chopin.

Structure du volume

Ce volume, dont la majeure partie est constituée des œuvres publiées après la disparition du compositeur, est organisé de la façon suivante : les huit premières Valses portant les numéros d'opus authentiques se succèdent par ordre chronologique de parution ; elles sont suivies par celles ayant été éditées après 1849, datant aussi bien de la période varsovienne que parisienne, qui sont rangées selon l'ordre chronologique de composition[4]. La Valse en La bémol majeur d'une authenticité douteuse (décrite à la page 246 du *Katalog* de Chomiński et Turło), et celle en Fa dièse mineur – d'une provenance encore plus incertaine (cf. *ibidem*, p. 250), ont été écartées.

Comme le démontre la liste des sources dressée dans le commentaire critique, la documentation est exceptionnellement abondante pour de nombreuses compositions de ce volume. Dans ces circonstances,

---

[1] Wilhelm von Lenz, *Uebersichtliche Beurtheilung der Pianoforte-Compositionen von Chopin, als Prodromus eines kritischen Katalogs seiner sämmtlichen Werke*, Neue Berliner Musikzeitung, 1872, nos 36–38. Sa traduction française est donnée dans l'*Annexe I* de la traduction éditée par Jean-Jacques Eigeldinger (voir la Bibliographie).

[2] Ce témoignage est sujet à caution, car, après avoir pris quelques leçons en 1842, Lenz n'a plus revu Chopin. Il est donc probable qu'il a mal interprété ce que l'un ou l'une des élèves de Chopin a voulu lui transmettre, c'est-à-dire que Chopin jouait les mesures introductives de cette valse dans un tempo *ad libitum*, en l'accélérant de plus en plus – d'où la métaphore du dévidement de la pelote.

[3] Pour plus de détails sur l'enseignement de cet élève tardif de Chopin voir l'ouvrage d'Aline Tasset, *La main et l'âme au piano d'après Schiffmacher* (Paris : Delagrave, 1908), ainsi que le livre de Jean-Jacques Eigeldinger, *Chopin vu par ses élèves* (Paris : Fayard, 2006), p. 124, 205–206 (note 231)). La 'tradition' d'arpègement dans l'opus 64 no 2, décrite d'une façon imprécise par Tasset (le fa double dièse ne peut être exécuté de la même façon que l'anacrouse sol dièse, c'est-à-dire sur le troisième temps), sur laquelle Jean-Jacques Eigeldinger émet certaines réserves, trouve probablement son origine dans l'opus 34 no 1 (cf. p. 108–114, version d'après **A¹** : mes. 17, 18, 20–22, 25, 26, 29, 30 *et seq.*) où les sixtes sont également arpégées.

[4] Ce classement exclut la numérotation d'opus « 66–74 » venant d'Adolphe-Martin Schlesinger (éditeur allemand des œuvres posthumes de Chopin), indûment attribué à Fontana, qui fait encore autorité. Quant aux dates de composition retenues, dont certaines suscitent toujours des polémiques, elles proviennent du *Katalog* de Chomiński et Turło (voir la Bibliographie).

en préparant le texte des valses dites « posthumes », il nous a semblé préférable d'accorder la priorité aux autographes de Chopin, plutôt que de recourir aux versions publiées par Julian Fontana, qui, depuis 1855 et pratiquement jusqu'à nos jours, constituent une référence incontournable pour la quasi-totalité des éditions critiques. Dans la nôtre, excepté un cas unique – la Valse en Ré bémol majeur, pour laquelle aucun manuscrit n'a été conservé –, l'édition de Fontana est considérée comme une source secondaire et n'est citée que si elle comporte des variantes susceptibles d'être authentiques et n'apparaissant nulle part ailleurs.

Une autre particularité de la présente publication réside dans l'exploitation des sources. Constitué souvent de plusieurs autographes reflétant des étapes décisives de la création, ce corpus mérite une place très supérieure à celle que lui est accordée dans la plupart des éditions modernes. Contrairement à une opinion encore répandue, ces documents ne sont pas destinés uniquement aux musicologues ; ils apportent des connaissances qui s'avèrent aussi très utiles aux interprètes en quête d'une interprétation respectueuse des intentions du compositeur. En livrant une image fascinante de l'évolution de l'œuvre dans ses moindres détails, ils montrent une face plus humaine du créateur dans sa recherche incessante de perfection – précision dans l'écriture – qui, toujours, est riche d'enseignements.

La quantité importante des versions impose une sélection et une organisation :
- Opus 18, 34 n° 1 et 64 n°^{s} 1 & 2 : les versions antérieures à celles livrées aux éditeurs sont situées dans l'Annexe. La séparation entre les deux catégories nous a paru nécessaire. Pour la première pièce de l'opus 64, les variantes provenant des trois autographes ont été réunies dans une version de synthèse, afin de faciliter la comparaison entre les sources
- les différentes versions des valses parues après 1849 se succèdent dans le corpus principal du volume. Faute de connaître les préférences du compositeur, ces versions doivent être considérées comme équivalentes. L'interprète est libre de choisir celle d'entre elles qui lui convient le mieux. Pour deux œuvres : Valses en La bémol majeur et en Fa mineur, dont les sources sont en nombre élevé, la démarche éditoriale a été similaire à celle décrite pour l'opus 64

n° 1. Une troisième version est proposée pour deux valses (en Si mineur et en Fa mineur) ; elle comporte le texte provenant de la première édition polonaise (1852) qui se fonde sur un manuscrit aujourd'hui perdu

Plusieurs de ces versions ont été divulguées par Edouard Ganche (1930), Alicja Simon (1949), Heinrich Neuhaus et Yakov Milstein (1953), Byron Janis (1978) ; la plupart des éditions Urtext n'en proposent qu'un choix limité. La lecture du texte de la Valse en La bémol majeur op. 34 n° 1 d'après le manuscrit de 1835, inclus dans l'album des sœurs Thun Hohenstein, s'avère particulièrement difficile en raison de la qualité insuffisante des reproductions mises au service des chercheurs. Avant que ce document perdu dans la tourmente de la seconde guerre mondiale ne soit retrouvé, aucune édition de cette version, y compris la nôtre, ne pourra être qualifiée de définitive.

Bibliographie

EIGELDINGER, JEAN-JACQUES, *Chopin vu par ses élèves* (Paris : Fayard, 2006)

GRABOWSKI, CHRISTOPHE & RINK, JOHN, *Annotated Catalogue of Chopin's First Editions* (Cambridge: CUP, 2010)

GUIGNARD, SILVAIN, *Frédéric Chopins Walzer. Eine text- und stilkritische Studie* (Baden-Baden : Koerner, 1986)

KOBYLAŃSKA, KRYSTYNA, *Rękopisy utworów Chopina – Katalog* (Kraków : PWM, 1977)

VON LENZ, WILHELM, *Les grands virtuoses du piano : Liszt, Chopin, Tausig, Henselt*, traduit et présenté par Jean-Jacques Eigeldinger (Paris : Flammarion, 1995)

RUHLMANN, SOPHIE, 'Chopin – Franchomme', *Chopin w kręgu przyjaciół*, vol. II (Warszawa : Neriton, 1996)

SCHUMANN, ROBERT, *Gesammelte Schriften über Musik und Musiker* (Leipzig : Breitkopf & Härtel, 1891)

TOMASZEWSKI, WOJCIECH, *Bibliografia warszawskich druków muzycznych 1801–1850* (Warszawa : Biblioteka Narodowa, 1992)

Christophe Grabowski

VORWORT*

Chopin und der Walzer

Wenn die uns vorliegenden Informationen richtig sind, finden sich Walzer sowohl im Früh- wie auch im Spätwerk von Frédéric Chopin. Die vor 1825 komponierten und im Album der Gräfin Izabella Grabowska enthaltenen Walzer scheinen endgültig verschollen zu sein. Von sieben anderen zwischen 1826 und 1830 komponierten Stücken wissen wir nur durch die von Ludwika Jędrzejewicz kurz nach dem Tod ihres Bruders erstellten Incipits. Vom letzten Walzer, den Chopin Katherine Erskine im Oktober 1848 gewidmet hat, ist nur noch die Nachbildung des Titelblatts vorhanden.

Abgesehen von Chopins Vorliebe für Tanzformen gehörte der Walzer zu den Gattungen, die ihm wohl seit seiner Kindheit ganz besonders vertraut gewesen waren. Schließlich war Warschau um 1810, wie andere europäische Hauptstädte auch, dem Charme des Walzers erlegen, der Schritt für Schritt die traditionellen Tänze verdrängt hatte. Lediglich der Mazur und die *Polonaise* konnten sich dieser Entwicklung widersetzen. Laut der Bibliographie von Wojciech Tomaszewski erschien der erste gedruckte Walzer in Chopins Heimat im Jahre 1815. In diesem Jahr endete auch der Wiener Kongresses, durch den der Walzer „geadelt" worden war. Mit Ausnahme des sehr ernsten Józef Elsner beginnen ab diesem Zeitpunkt alle polnischen Komponisten damit, im Walzer-Rhythmus zu komponieren. Seine wichtigste und ganz am Zweck orientierte Aufgabe dabei ist

es, dass man nach ihm tanzen kann: bei Bällen oder abendlichen Tanzveranstaltungen, die in einem privaten, ja familiären Rahmen stattfinden. Bei einem solchen Anlass wird ihn auch der junge Frédéric kennen gelernt haben. Die oben genannten Incipits jedenfalls verweisen auf eine gänzlich unprätentiöse Musik, die lediglich dem Tanzvergnügen dienen sollte.

Doch sollte Chopin durch zwei Reisen nach Wien seine Meinung ändern. Zwar gesteht er dem Walzer keinen künstlerischen Wert zu, wie folgendes ironische Zitat aus einem Brief an Elsner vom 29. Januar 1831 zeigt: „Hier werden Walzer als Werke bezeichnet und man nennt Strauss und Lanner, die sie zum Tanz spielen, ‚Kapellmeister'!" – was ihn aber nicht daran hindert, genau in dieser Stadt einen Walzer zu komponieren. Über diese, uns unbekannte Komposition informiert er seine Familie in einem Brief vom 22. Dezember 1830. Bezeichnenderweise bemerkt er darin aber auch, dass er seine gerade erst komponierten Mazurken nicht länger als „für den Tanz komponiert" bezeichnen wolle. Seine Meinung zum Walzer sollte sich zu einem späteren Zeitpunkt, dann aber in Paris, in gleicher Weise ändern.

Fünf Walzer stammen aus der Zeit zwischen 1829 und 1830. Der schwung- und temperamentvolle Walzer in As-Dur (der einzige in einem $\frac{3}{8}$-Takt) ist in seinem Charakter noch als Volkstanz angelegt und fest in der Funktion als Tanzstück verankert. Im Gegensatz dazu

---

* Zu ganz besonderem Dank bin ich Jean-Jacques Eigeldinger und John Rink für ihre wertvollen Textanmerkungen verpflichtet.

tragen die Walzer in E-Dur, h-Moll, Des-Dur und e-Moll schon eher Chopins persönliche Handschrift, da bei ihnen erstmals das lyrische Element stärker hervorgehoben wird. Bei einem dieser Stücke gibt der jugendliche Chopin – ganz ungewöhnlich – die Quelle seiner Inspiration preis, nämlich sein durch die junge Sängerin Konstancja Gładkowska verkörpertes Ideal. Im Begleitbrief zum Manuskript des Walzers in Des-Dur lenkt er die Aufmerksamkeit seines Freundes und Vertrauten Tytus Woyciechowski auf einen mit einem Kreuz gekennzeichneten Takt: Es handelt sich dabei um die Stelle, an welcher der Überschwang der Gefühle seinen Höhepunkt erreichen soll.

Von den zwölf Walzern, die Chopin nach seinem Umzug nach Paris komponiert hatte, wurden lediglich acht von ihm selbst veröffentlicht. Ein Vergleich der verschiedenen Fassungen von op. 18, 34, Nr. 1 und op. 64, Nr. 1 & 2 zeigt deutlich, welchen Fortschritt Chopin in der Ausführung gemacht hat. Eine Stelle in der Korrespondenz von Auguste Franchomme an Jules Forest verweist auf den genauen Zeitpunkt, an dem die Coda in op. 18 eingefügt wurde, nämlich erst am Tag der endgültigen Fertigstellung der Stichvorlage. Die finale Ausgestaltung der zweiten genannten Komposition verlief in ähnlicher Weise, da auch hier die Coda erst in der endgültigen Fassung zum ersten Mal erscheint. Ein aufmerksamer Blick auf die fertiggestellte Stichvorlage des Walzers op. 64, Nr. 1 genügt, um festzustellen, dass die Schlusspassage als Tonleiter erst äußerst spät hinzugefügt wurde – eine Verbesserung, die bei den vier nicht für die Veröffentlichung zurückgehaltenen Walzern (Nr. 15–18) fehlt. Diese sind allesamt mit einem unveränderlichen da capo versehen. Letztere gehören zu einer Kategorie von ganz persönlichen Werken mit melancholischem Charakter (mit Ausnahme des ältesten Stückes in Ges-Dur, bei dem vergnügte Unbekümmertheit, gepaart mit einem Hauch Sanftheit, noch uneingeschränkt vorherrscht). Chopin widmete diese Stücke Freunden und Schülern und wünschte nicht, dass sie allgemein bekannt gemacht würden. Das legt er ganz klar in einem Brief an Caroline de Belleville-Oury fest, eine der Empfängerinnen eines Manuskripts des f-Moll-Walzers.

Chopin bezeichnet keinen seiner Walzer als *groß*, *brillant* oder *melancholisch*. Manche dieser allesamt von Herausgebern stammenden Bezeichnungen stehen sogar im krassen Gegensatz zum Charakter von op. 34, Nr. 2, das genau wie die beiden anderen Werke unter dieser Opuszahl von Maurice Schlesinger als *Grande Valse brillante* bezeichnet wurde. Christian Rudolph Wessel, der für seine fantasievollen Titel bekannt war, bezeichnete op. 18 als *Invitation pour la danse* und erinnerte damit an Carl Maria von Webers berühmte *Aufforderung zum Tanz* op. 65.

Robert Schumann war einer der ersten, die den wahren Wert von Chopins Walzern erkannten, als er sie als die besten Werke dieser Gattung bezeichnete und gleichzeitig betonte, wie unnachahmlich sie – genau wie Chopins übrige Werke – seien. Für ihn war Chopins op. 42 von höchst aristokratischem Charakter und um diese Einschätzung zu untermauern ließ er Florestan – einem seiner literarischen *Alter Ego* – mitteilen, dass, wenn man diese Walzer bei einem Ball spielte, „so müssten unter den Tänzerinnen die gute Hälfte wenigstens Comtessen sein".

Der Walzer vor und nach Chopin

Die Mitte des 19. Jahrhunderts markiert die Blütezeit dieser Tanzform, deren Ursprünge jedoch wesentlich weiter zurückreichen. Ohne bis zu den eigentlichen, sicherlich im Volkstanz zu findenden Ursprüngen zurückgehen noch den spektakulären Aufstieg des Walzers vom ländlichen Fest bis in die Salons der Aristokratie nachzeichnen zu wollen, soll es hier genügen festzuhalten, dass die ältesten Walzer aus zwei jeweils achttaktigen Perioden bestanden. In der weiteren Entwicklung wurden die beiden Teile immer länger und im Charakter zunehmend kontrastierend gestaltet. Dann kam eine Reprise hinzu und schließlich als Einschnitt ein *da capo* mit *Trio* – ganz wie dies bei Chopin zu finden ist. Die höchste Entwicklungsstufe fand diese Form in der *Aufforderung zum Tanz* von Weber, die aus einer ganzen Reihe von Walzern besteht, welche von Introduktion und Coda eingerahmt sind. In so manchem Walzer aus seiner Pariser Zeit nimmt Chopin auf eben diese Form Bezug.

Die Liste der Komponisten, die sich von dieser Tanzform angezogen fühlten, ist äußerst lang. Im Bereich der Klaviermusik sind die *Tanzcomponisten* Legion: Ihre einstmals gefeierten Werke füllen heute ganze Bibliotheken. Die Walzer von Schubert und Beethoven stehen stellvertretend für die ersten beiden Entwicklungsstufen und sind aufgrund der Berühmtheit ihrer Komponisten erhalten geblieben. Nicht vergessen werden sollte, dass eine der faszinierendsten Kompositionen des Bonner Meisters, nämlich die *33 Variationen*, op. 120, thematisch auf einem belanglosen Walzer von Diabelli beruhen. Von Chopins Zeitgenossen verstand es allein Franz Liszt, mit dieser Tanzform neue Horizonte zu erschließen, indem er mit seinem diabolischen *Mephisto-Walzer* die Virtuosität auf ein bis heute unerreichtes Niveau hob. Johannes Brahms als Komponist der nachfolgenden Generation verleiht seinem Opus 39, einer Reihe von Walzern zu 4 Händen, vornehme Ausdrucksstärke und transkribiert das Werk sogar selbst für Klavier zu 2 Händen. Die *Valses-Caprices* von Gabriel Fauré erreichen dagegen nicht das hohe Niveau seiner Nocturnes oder Barcarolles, und nur einige wenige Geniestreiche blitzen in der *Etude en forme de Valse* von Camille Saint-Saëns auf. *La plus que lente* von Claude Debussy, vom Komponisten selbst auf Klavierrollen für die Nachwelt verewigt, ist mehr ein Pasticcio französischer Sentimentalität als eine Hommage an das Genre selbst, das zu Beginn des 20. Jahrhunderts bereits deutlich an Bedeutung verliert. Schließlich finden die wesentlichen Charaktereigenschaften der Tanzform meisterlichen Ausdruck in einem der letzten Juwelen pianistischer Literatur, die diesem Genre gewidmet sind, den *Valses nobles et sentimentales* von Maurice Ravel.

Was das Orchesterrepertoire betrifft, sind Johann Strauss und seine drei Söhne mit ihren unsterblichen Walzern, die alle Facetten des Wiener Lebens musikalisch beleuchten, an erster Stelle zu nennen. Walzer erklingen auch in der symphonischen Musik von Berlioz, Tschaikowsky, Mahler und Shostakovich, in den Opern von Gounod, Tschaikowsky, Offenbach, Massenet, Leoncavallo, Puccini, R. Strauss, Berg, ja selbst in Wagners Parsifal. Immer wieder ist der Walzer in zahllosen Operetten und praktisch jeder Ballettmusik des 19. und frühen 20. Jahrhunderts zu hören. Maurice Ravel war einer der letzten, der dem Walzer mit seinem choreographischen Gedicht *La Valse* von 1920 huldigte und damit diesem Tanz zu seiner Apotheose verhalf.

Zur Aufführung von Walzern

Es existieren Berichte über Chopins Improvisationen von Mazurken und anderen Tänzen (mit großer Sicherheit Walzer) bei privaten Soireen in Warschau und Paris. Seine Walzer waren auch bei seinem letzten Konzert in Paris und ebenso bei öffentlichen Auftritten in England und Schottland im Jahre 1848 zu hören.

In seiner *Uebersichtlichen Beurtheilung*[1], berichtet Wilhelm von Lenz, dass Chopin den Walzer op. 42 „als continuierliche Stretta-*Prestissimo* mit Beibehaltung des Tactes in den Bässen" ausführte und das Werk nach seinen Angaben „spieluhrenartig" zu geben sei. Weiterhin berichtet er, dass Chopin im ersten Walzer op. 64 „aus den ersten 4 Tacten annähernd 2" machte[2], „das sein abzuwickeln wie ein

---

[1] Wilhelm von Lenz, *Uebersichtliche Beurtheilung der Pianoforte-Compositionen von Chopin, als Prodromus eines kritischen Katalogs seiner sämmtlichen Werke*, Neue Berliner Musikzeitung, 1872, Nr. 36–38.

[2] Dieser Bericht über op. 64 ist mit Vorsicht zu genießen, da Lenz nach einigen Unterrichtsstunden im Jahre 1842 Chopin nie mehr wiedergesehen hat. Es ist daher anzunehmen, dass er das, was ihm von einem Schüler Chopins berichtet wurde, falsch interpretiert hat, d.h. dass Chopin die Einführungstakte dieses Walzers in freiem Tempo, also *ad libitum*, und dann immer schneller werdend gespielt hat (daher auch die Metapher eines sich abwickelnden Knäuels).

Knäul", so der Komponist. Die Tempoangabe bezog sich lediglich auf den Bass im fünften Takt. Lenz behauptet in ähnlicher Weise, dass Chopin in op. 64, Nr. 2 kaum zufrieden zu stellen gewesen sei und dass „nur er verstand, das eine Sechszehntheil (im 3ten Tact) dem darauf folgenden Virtelwerth zu verbinden!".

Die von Joseph Schiffmacher überlieferten und wahrscheinlich vom Komponisten stammenden Ratschläge zur nuancierten und leichten Ausführung der dritten Taktteile in der Begleitung der linken Hand sowie der Vorschlag zum Arpeggieren der Sexte in der rechten Hand im zweiten Takt op. 64, Nr. 2, sind ebenfalls erhalten[3].

Was die Ausführung von Werken betrifft, die in mehreren Fassungen vorliegen oder für die eine zusammenfassende Version vorgeschlagen wird, empfiehlt der Herausgeber mit Nachdruck, sich möglichst für nur eine einzelne Quelle zu entscheiden. Die jeweiligen Varianten stellen in ihrer Gesamtheit eine übergeordnete Logik dar, die beim ersten Lesen häufig übersehen wird. Die Verschmelzung verschiedener Fassungen wird nur erfahrenen Interpreten empfohlen, die mit den Besonderheiten des Chopinschen Kompositionsprozesses vertraut sind.

Aufbau der Ausgabe

Die vorliegende Ausgabe enthält zum größten Teil Werke, die nach dem Tod des Komponisten veröffentlicht wurden, und ist wie folgt gegliedert: Die acht ersten Walzer sind mit originalen Opuszahlen versehen und chronologisch nach dem Datum ihrer Veröffentlichung geordnet. Es folgen die nach 1849 herausgegebenen Werke, die aus Chopins Zeit in Warschau und Paris stammen und chronologisch nach dem Zeitpunkt ihrer Komposition geordnet sind[4]. Die Authentizität des Walzers in As-Dur ist umstritten (vgl. *Katalog* von Chomiński und Turło, Seite 246), und die Herkunft des Walzers in fis-Moll ist noch weniger geklärt (vgl. *ibidem*, S. 250). Daher wurden diese Werke nicht mit aufgenommen.

Wie die Liste der Quellen, die im kritischen Bericht aufgeführt sind, zeigt, gibt es eine ungewöhnlich große Zahl von Dokumenten zu verschiedenen in diesem Band enthaltenen Kompositionen. Unter diesen Umständen erschien es uns bei der Einrichtung der als „posthum" bezeichneten Walzer sinnvoll, den Autographen Chopins den Vorzug zu geben vor den von Julian Fontana veröffentlichten Fassungen, die seit 1855 und praktisch bis zum heutigen Tag als Referenz für fast alle kritischen Editionen gilt. In dieser Ausgabe wird die Fontana-Fassung lediglich als Sekundärquelle genutzt, und dies nur dann, wenn sie Varianten enthält, die aller Wahrscheinlichkeit nach authentisch und nicht an anderer Stelle zu finden sind. Ausgenommen hiervon ist nur der Walzer in Des-Dur, von dem kein Manuskript erhalten geblieben ist.

Eine weitere Besonderheit der vorliegenden Ausgabe besteht in der Auswertung der Quellen. Da diese häufig aus mehreren Autographen bestehen, die wiederum verschiedene Schaffensperioden repräsentieren, wird diesem Korpus ein wesentlich höherer Stellenwert eingeräumt als dies in den meisten modernen Ausgaben der Fall ist. Im Gegensatz zu einer weit verbreiteten Meinung sind diese Dokumente nicht ausschließlich für Musikwissenschaftler bestimmt. Vielmehr enthalten sie auch nützliche Informationen für den Interpreten, der bestrebt ist, den Intentionen des Komponisten respektvoll nachzuspüren. Dabei zeichnen sie ein faszinierendes Bild von der Entwicklung des Werkes in seinen kleinsten Details und zeigen die menschliche Seite des Komponisten bei seiner stetigen Suche nach Perfektion – der Präzision in der Notation. Damit stellen sie auch heute noch einen reichhaltigen Fundus an Informationen dar.

Die Vielzahl der verfügbaren Fassungen machte eine Auswahl und Gliederung erforderlich:

- Op. 18, 34, Nr. 1 und 64, Nr. 1 & 2: Die zeitlich vor den hier genutzten Versionen liegenden Frühfassungen sind im Anhang aufgeführt. Die Aufteilung in diese beiden Kategorien erschien uns notwendig. Für das erste Stück von op. 64 wurden die aus drei Autographen entnommenen Varianten zu einer Version zusammengefasst, um den Vergleich zwischen den Quellen zu erleichtern.
- Die verschiedenen Fassungen der nach 1849 erschienenen Walzer folgen im Hauptkorpus der Ausgabe aufeinander. Da nicht bekannt ist, welche Fassung vom Komponisten bevorzugt wurde, sollen sie hier als gleichberechtigt angesehen werden. Dem Ausführenden ist es freigestellt, welche Fassung ihm am meisten zusagt. Bei zwei Werken, den Walzern in As-Dur und f-Moll, für die eine große Zahl von Quellen zur Verfügung steht, verfolgte der Herausgeber einen ähnlichen Ansatz wie für op. 64, Nr. 1. Für zwei Walzer (in h-Moll und f-Moll) ist eine dritte Fassung angegeben, die den Notentext der ersten polnischen Ausgabe enthält (1852), welche auf einem heute verschollenen Manuskript beruhte.

Mehrere dieser Fassungen fanden Verbreitung durch Edouard Ganche (1930), Alicja Simon (1949), Heinrich Neuhaus/Yakov Milstein (1953) und Byron Janis (1978); ihre, häufig eng eingegrenzte, Auswahl ist ebenfalls in den meisten Urtextausgaben enthalten. Das Lesen des Notentextes des Walzers in As-Dur op. 34, Nr. 1 nach dem Manuskript von 1835 aus dem Album der Schwestern Thun Hohenstein, erwies sich aufgrund der unzureichenden Qualität der den Forschern zur Verfügung stehenden Reproduktionen als besonders schwierig. Nachdem dieses Dokument in den Wirren des Zweiten Weltkriegs verloren ging und nicht mehr auffindbar ist, kann keine Ausgabe dieser Fassung, auch nicht die unsere, als endgültig angesehen werden.

Bibliographie

EIGELDINGER, JEAN-JACQUES, *Chopin vu par ses élèves* (Paris: Fayard, 2006)

GRABOWSKI, CHRISTOPHE & RINK, JOHN, *Annotated Catalogue of Chopin's First Editions* (Cambridge: CUP, 2010)

GUIGNARD, SILVAIN, *Frédéric Chopins Walzer. Eine text- und stilkritische Studie* (Baden-Baden: Koerner, 1986)

KOBYLAŃSKA, KRYSTYNA, *Rękopisy utworów Chopina* – Katalog (Kraków: PWM, 1977)

VON LENZ, WILHELM, *Les grands virtuoses du piano : Liszt, Chopin, Tausig, Henselt*, übersetzt und vorgestellt von Jean-Jacques Eigeldinger (Paris: Flammarion, 1995)

RUHLMANN, SOPHIE, 'Chopin – Franchomme', *Chopin w kręgu przyjaciół*, vol. II (Warszawa: Neriton, 1996)

SCHUMANN, ROBERT, *Gesammelte Schriften über Musik und Musiker* (Leipzig: Breitkopf & Härtel, 1891)

TOMASZEWSKI, WOJCIECH, *Bibliografia warszawskich druków muzycznych 1801–1850* (Warszawa: Biblioteka Narodowa, 1992)

Christophe Grabowski / Übersetzt von Holger Klier

---

[3] Weitere Details zum Unterricht dieses späten Schülers von Chopin finden sich in der Veröffentlichung von Aline Tasset, *La main et l'âme au piano d'après Schiffmacher* (Paris: Delagrave, 1908), sowie im Buch von Jean-Jacques Eigeldinger, *Chopin vu par ses élèves* (Paris: Fayard, 2006, S. 124 und 205–206). Die „Tradition" des Arpeggios in op. 64, Nr. 2, von Tasset nur wenig präzise beschrieben, (das fisis lässt sich nicht in gleicher Weise ausführen wie der Auftakt gis, d.h. auf die dritte Zählzeit), die Jean-Jacques Eigeldinger mit einer gewissen Zurückhaltung betrachtet, hat ihren Ursprung vermutlich in op. 34, Nr. 1 (vgl. S. 108–114, Fassung gemäß **A¹**: Takte 17, 18, 20–22, 25, 26, 29, 30 ff), bei welchem die Sexten ebenfalls arpeggiert werden.

[4] Diese Gliederung berücksichtigt nicht die Nummerierung der Werke „66–74", die auf den deutschen Herausgeber der posthumen Werke Chopins, Adolphe-Martin Schlesinger, zurückgeht (fälschlicherweise Fontana zugeschrieben) und nach wie vor Gültigkeit besitzt. Die zum Teil immer noch umstrittenen Kompositionsdaten sind dem *Katalog* von Chomiński und Turło entnommen (vgl. Bibliographie).

Grande Valse brillante, Op. 18

dédiée à Mlle Laura Horsford

★ See Critical Commentary.

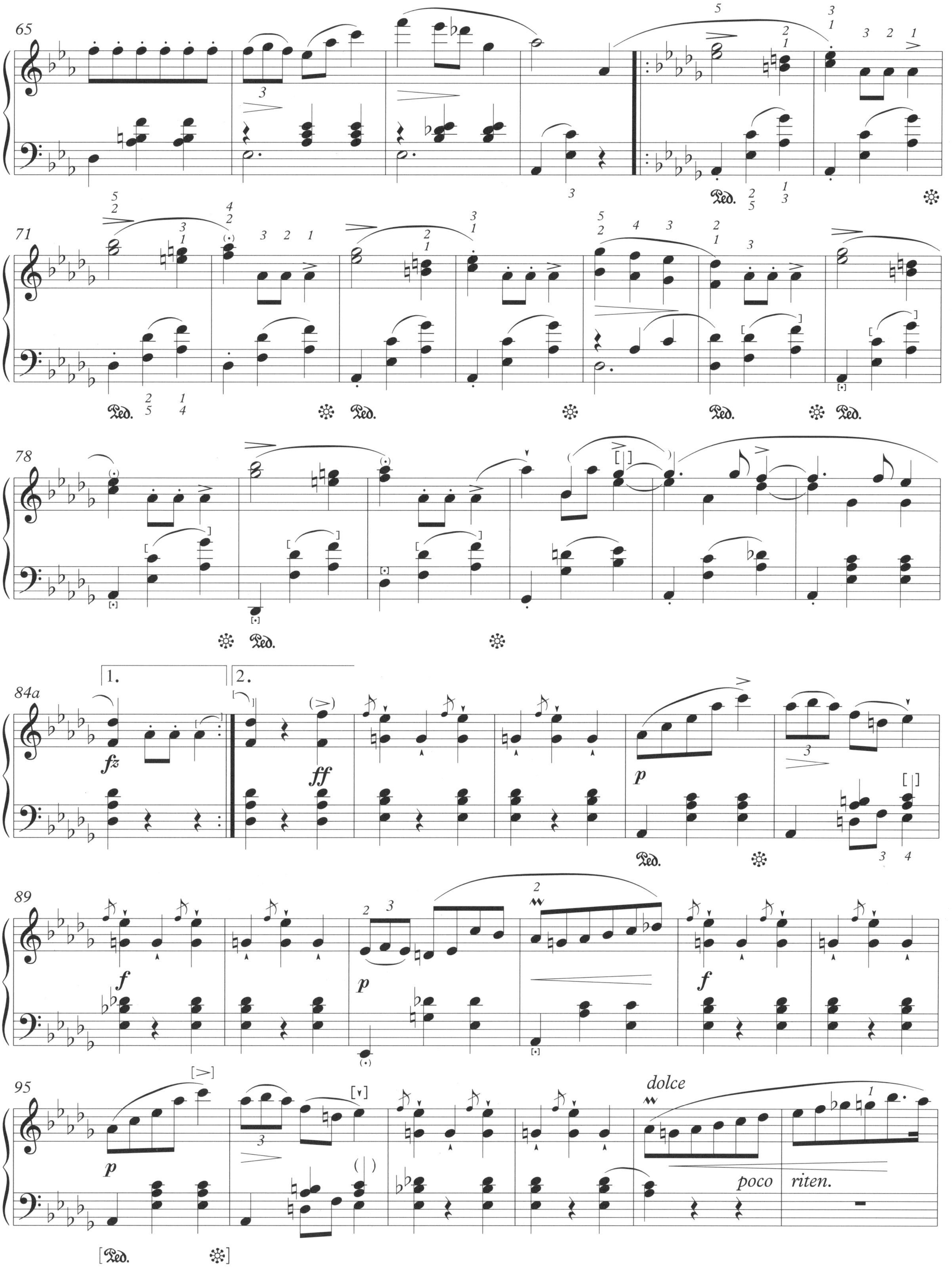
65
71
78
84a
1.
2.
89
95
dolce
poco
riten.
Ped.

★ See Critical Commentary.

Grande Valse brillante, Op. 34 No. 1

dédiée à Mlle J. de Thun-Hohenstein

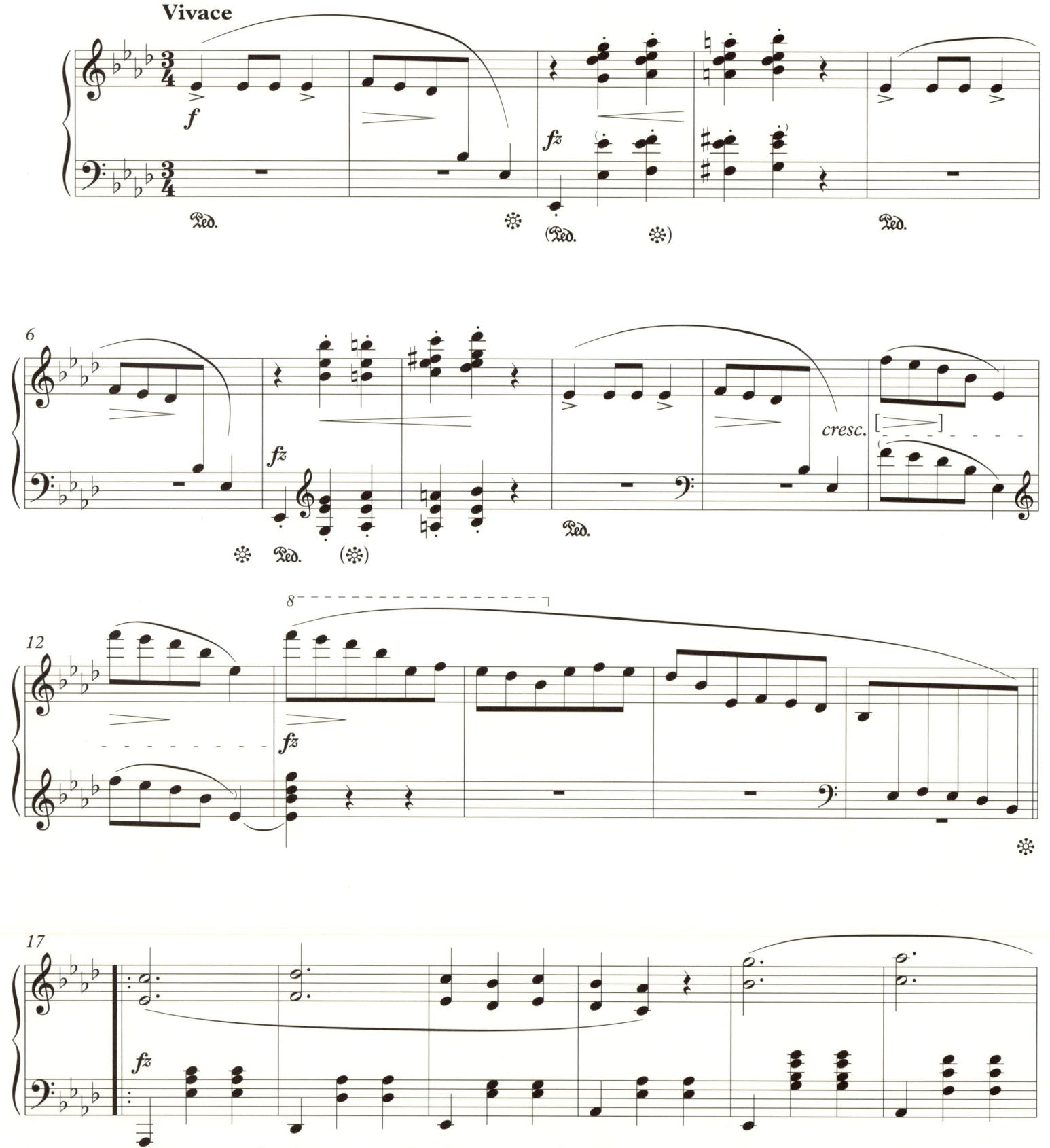

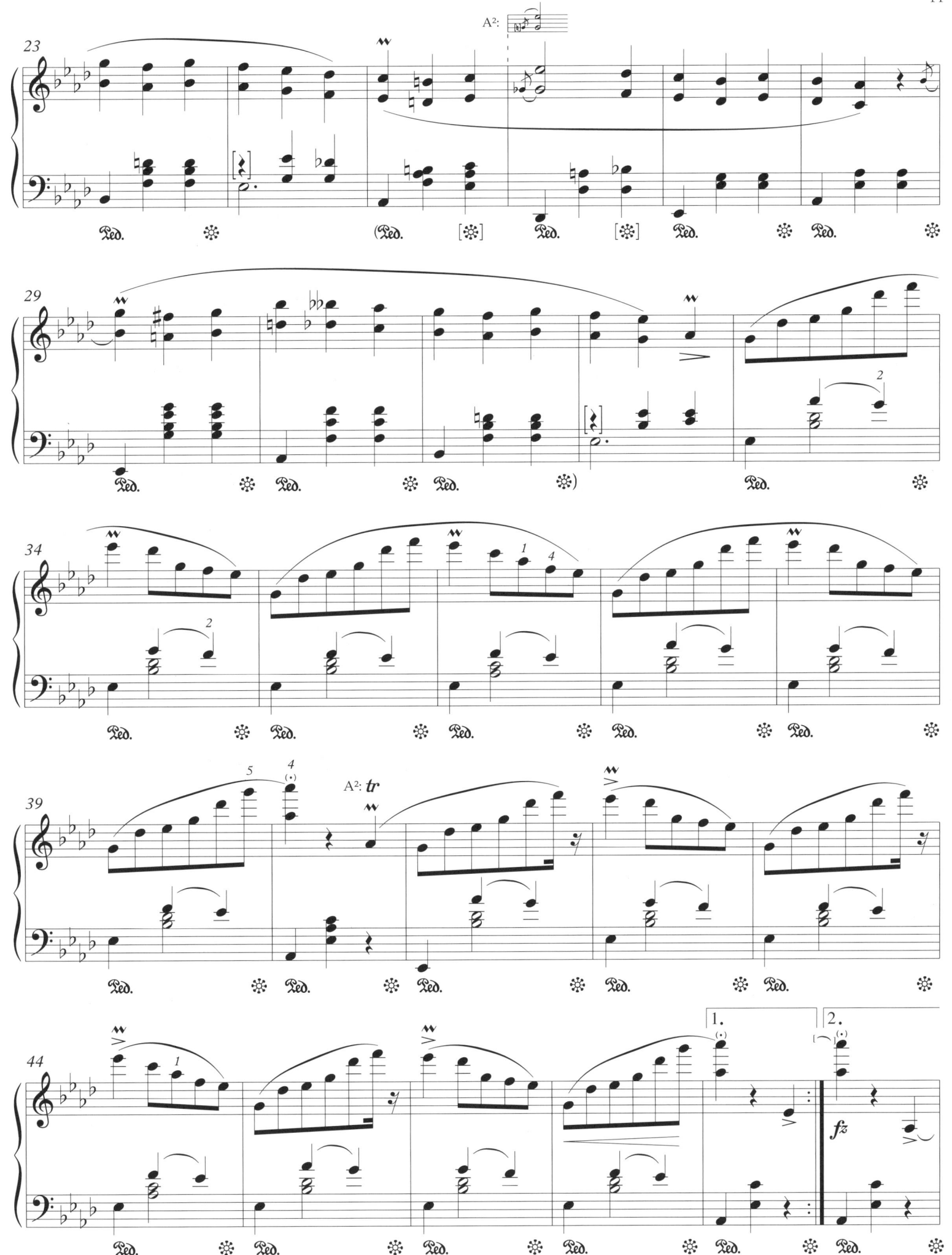

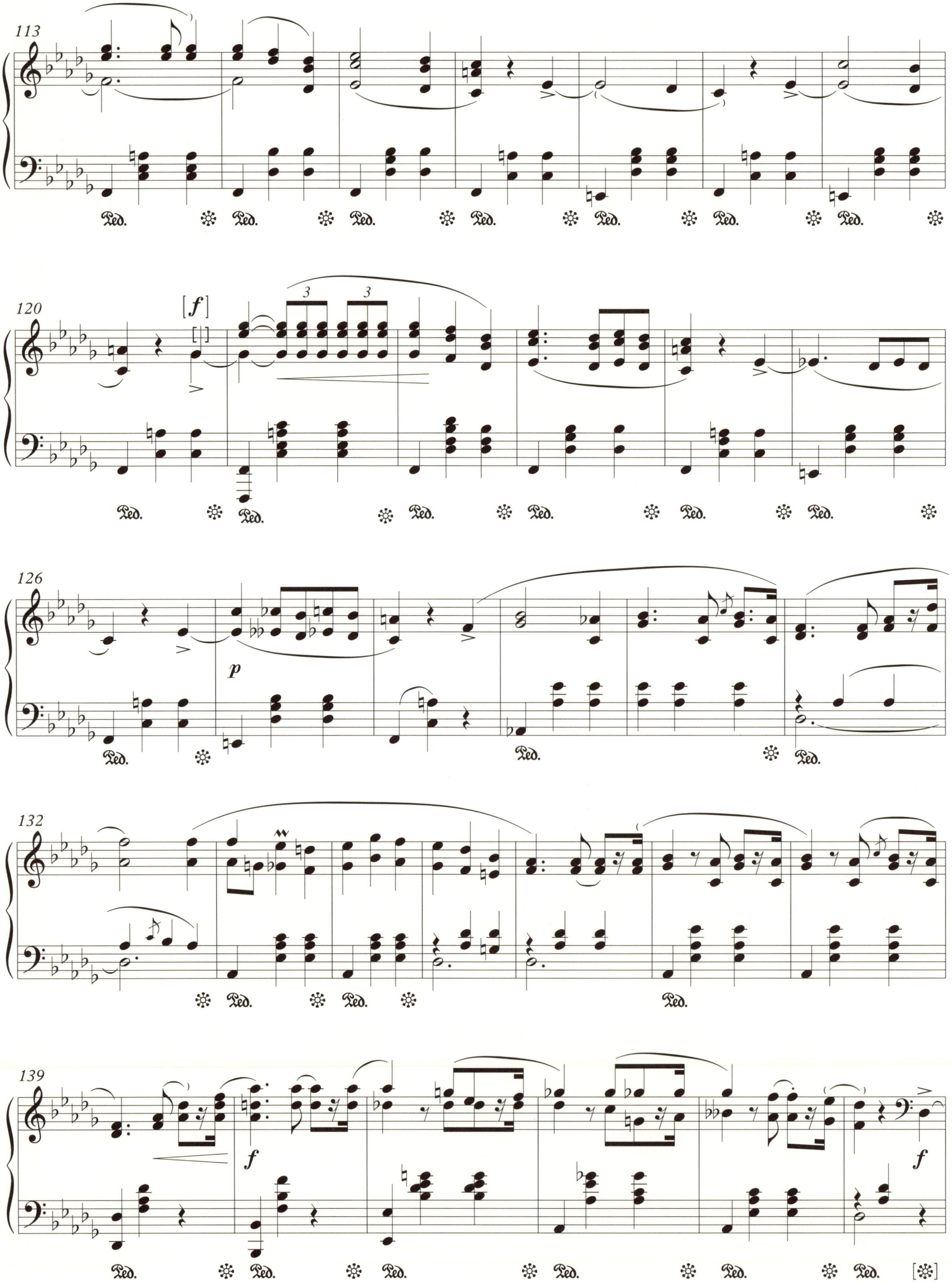
113
120
[f]
p
126
132
139
f
Ped.

Valse, Op. 34 No. 2

à Madame la Baronne C. d'Ivry

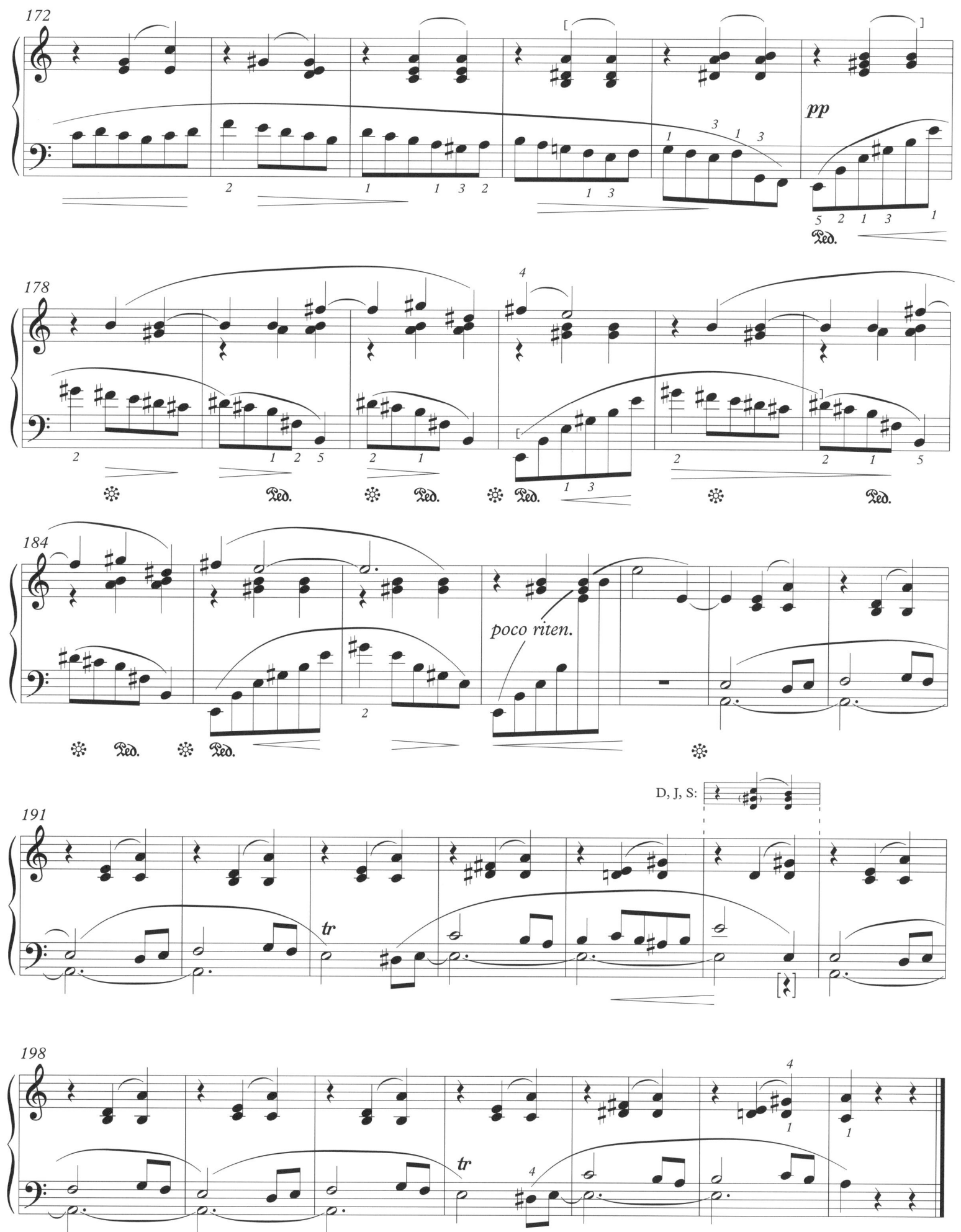

Grande Valse brillante, Op. 34 No. 3

à Mlle A. d'Eichtal

Valse, Op. 42

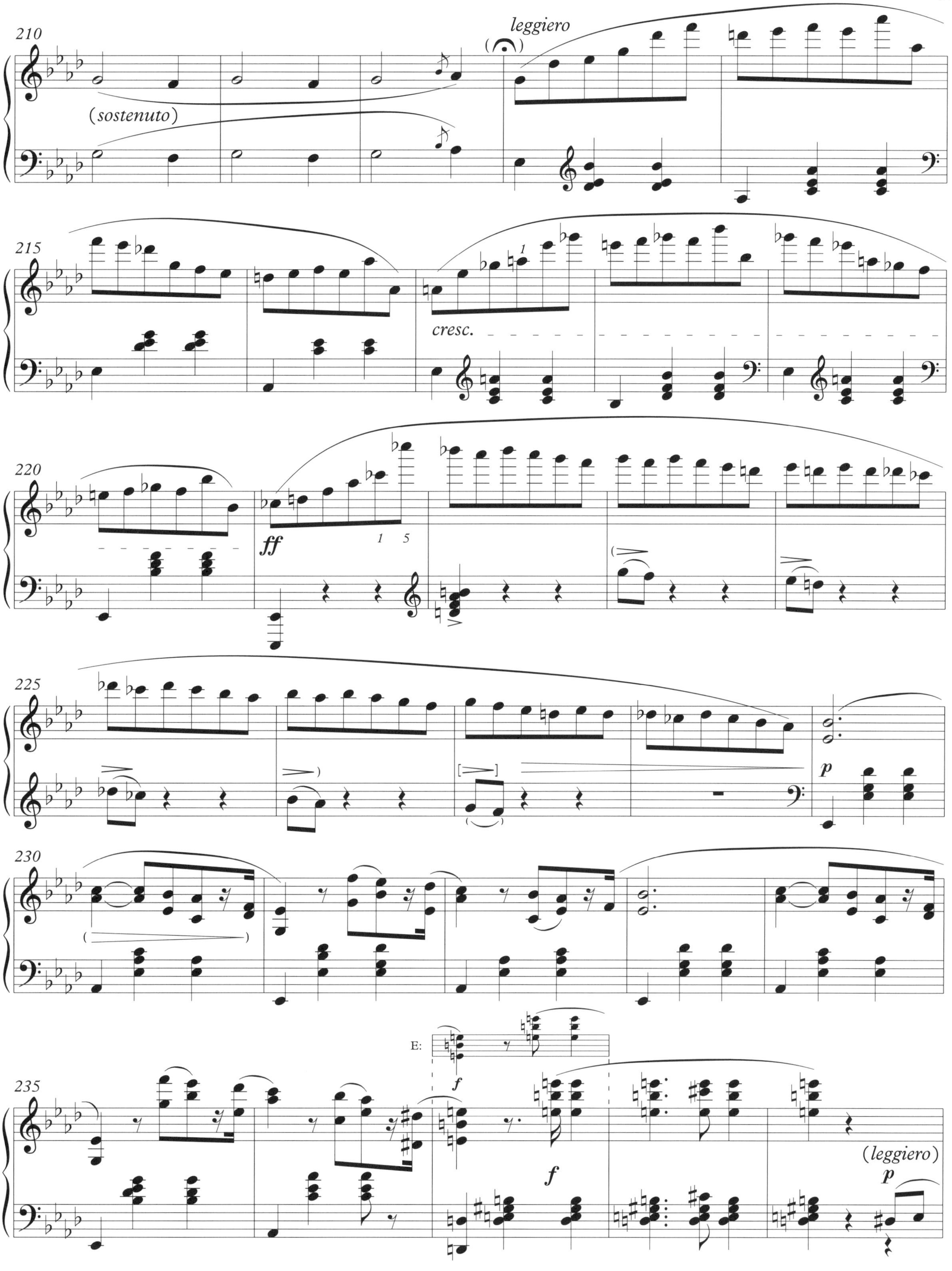
210
leggiero
(sostenuto)
215
cresc.
220
ff
225
p
230
235
E:
f
f
(leggiero)
p

★ Regarding dynamics, see Critical Commentary.

Valse, Op. 64 No. 1

à Madame la Comtesse Delphine Potocka

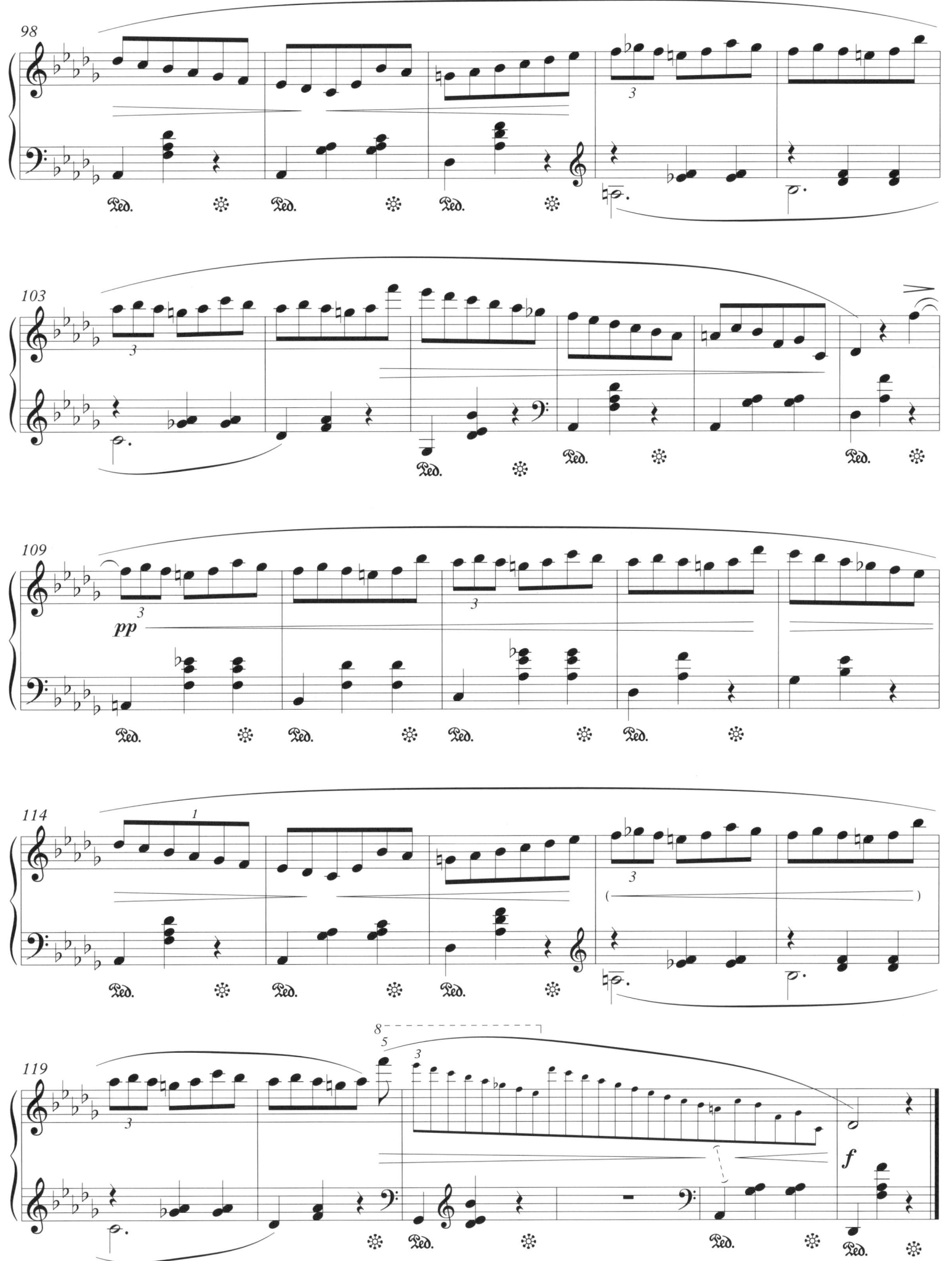

Valse, Op. 64 No. 2

à Madame la Baronne Nathaniel de Rothschild

Valse, Op. 64 No. 3

à Mademoiselle la Comtesse Catherine Branicka

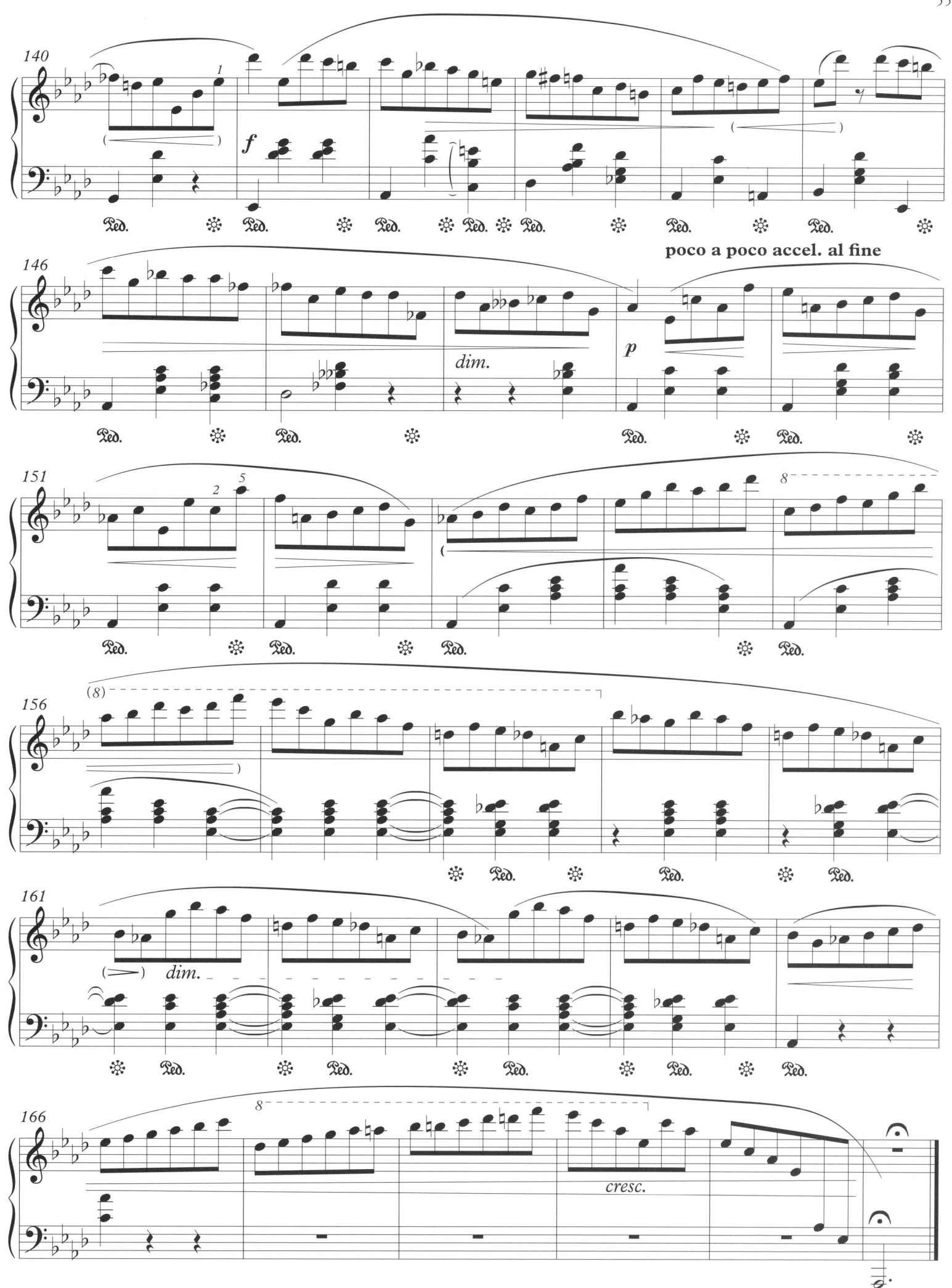

Valse

(Version based on **C¹**; see source information, p.134)

(Composed 1829)

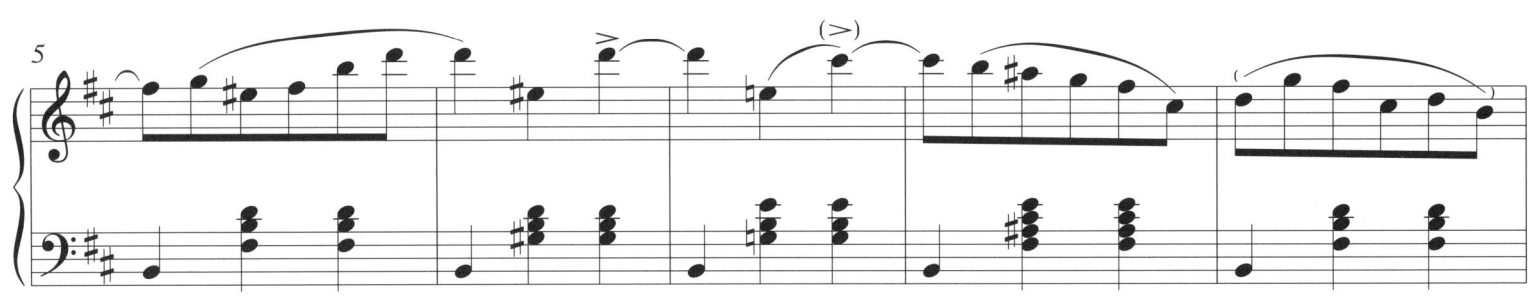
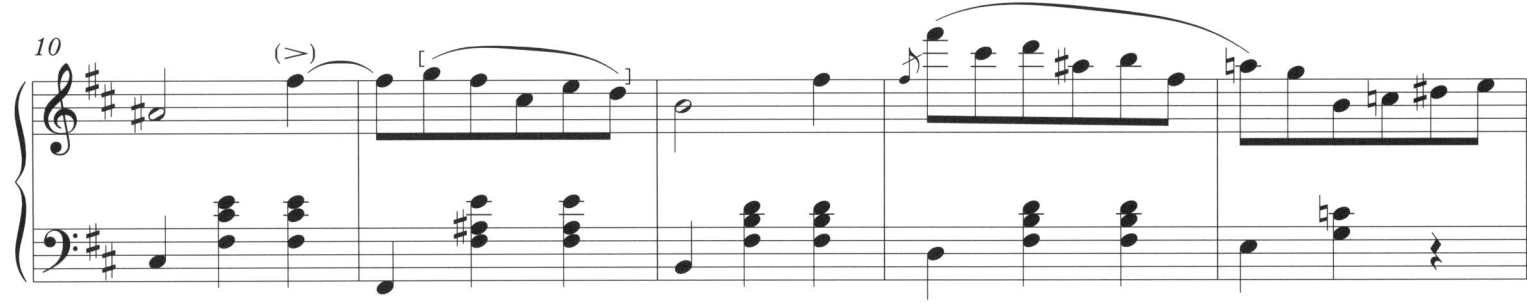

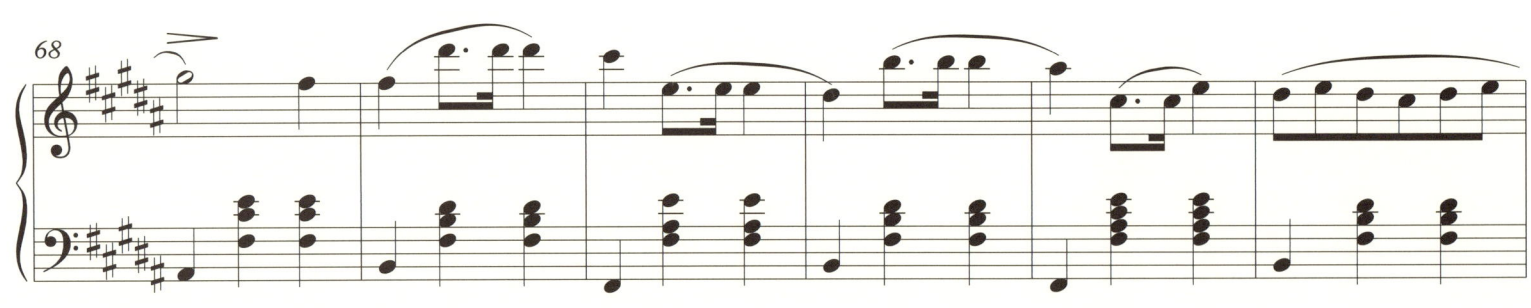

Valse

(Version based on C^2; see source information, p.134)

Valse

(Version based on **P**; see source information, p.134)

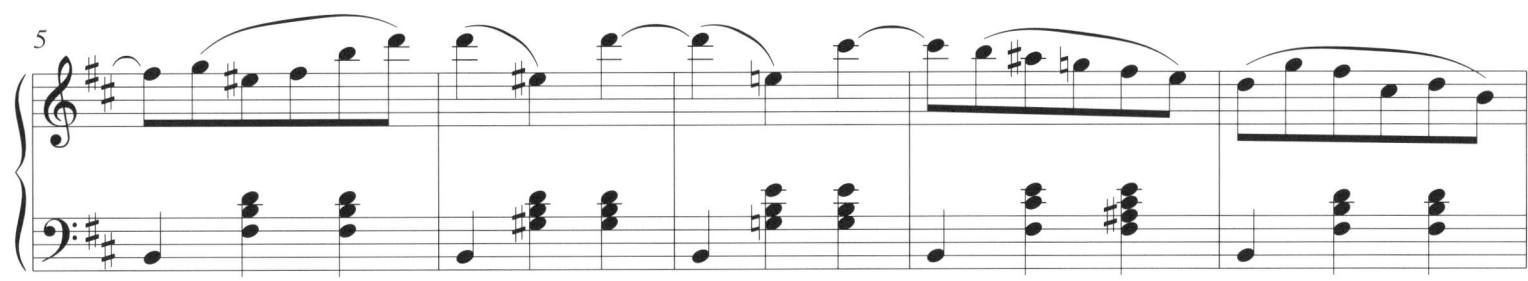

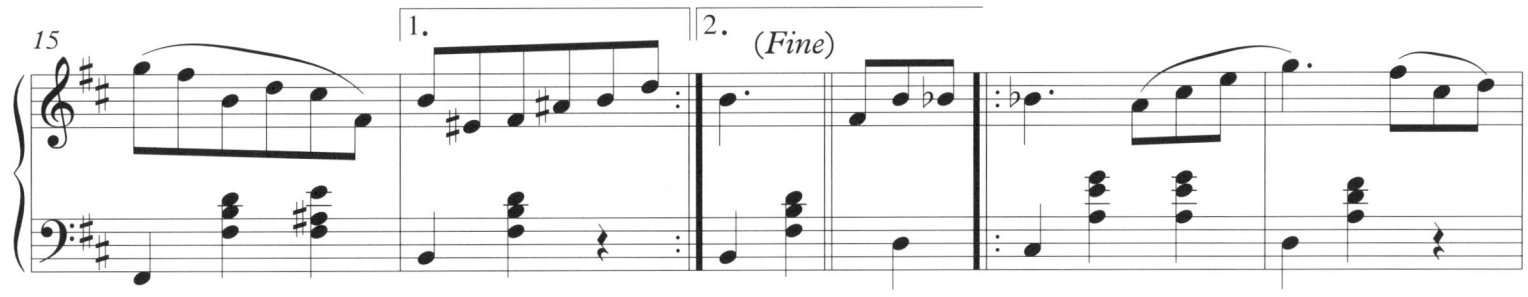

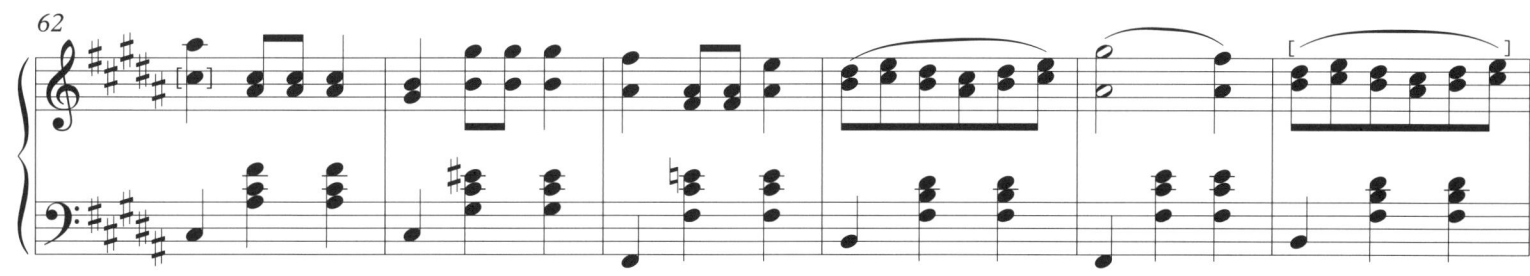
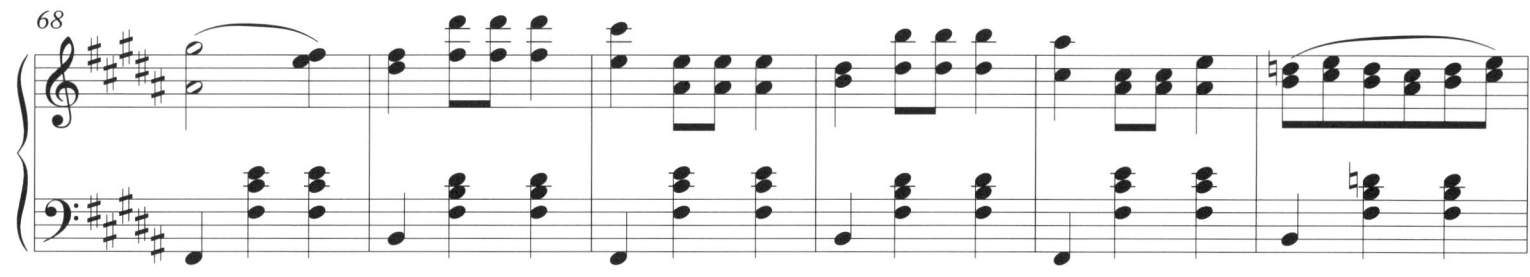

Valse

(Composed 1829)

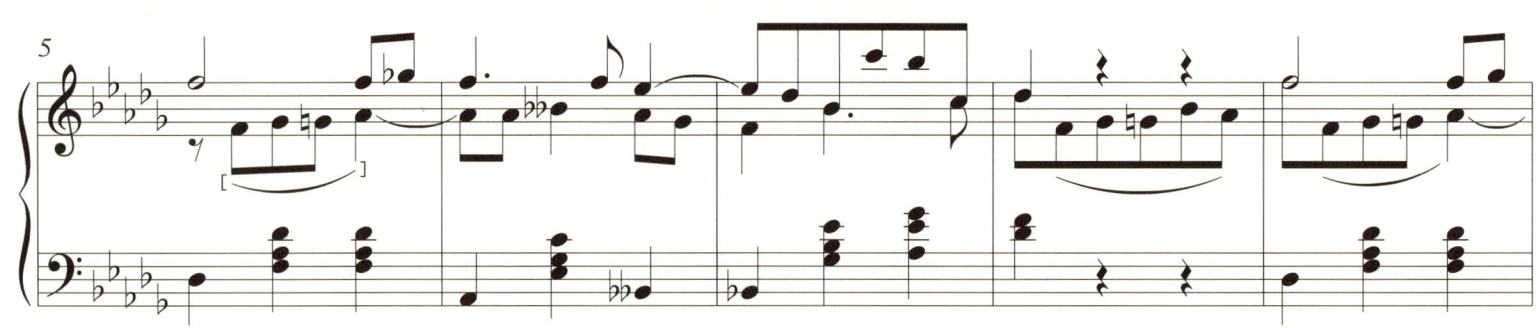
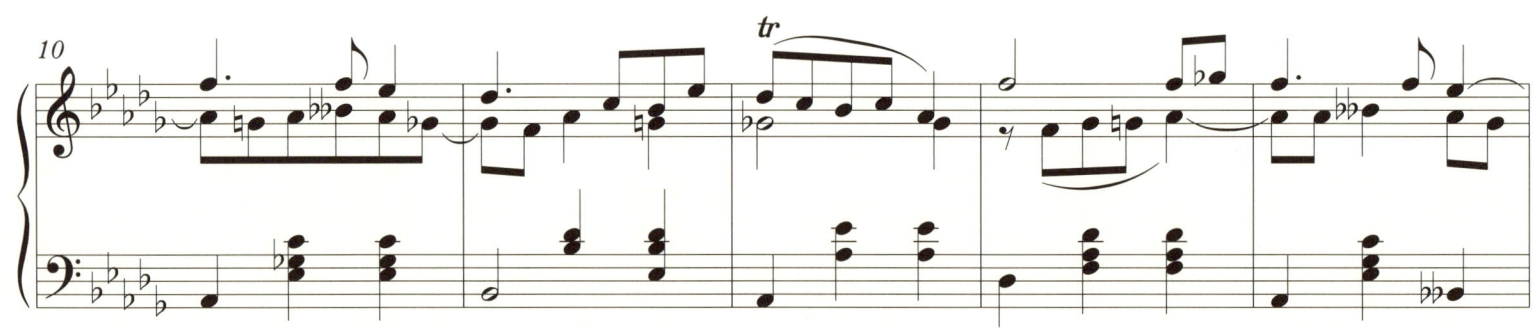

★ See Critical Commentary.

Valse

(Composed 1829/30)

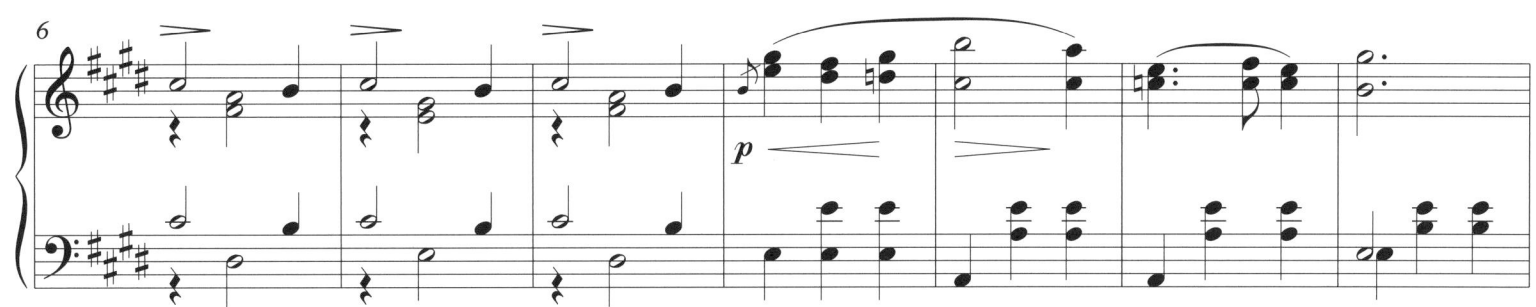
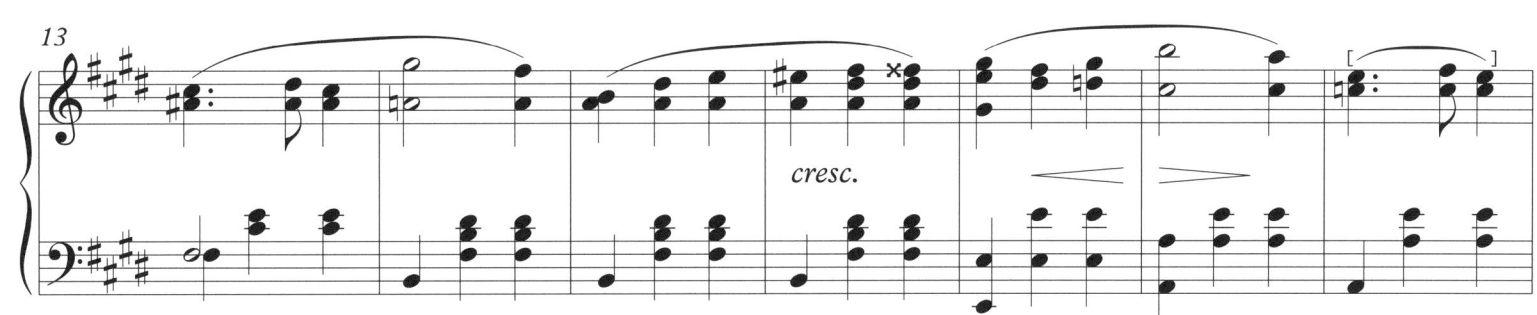
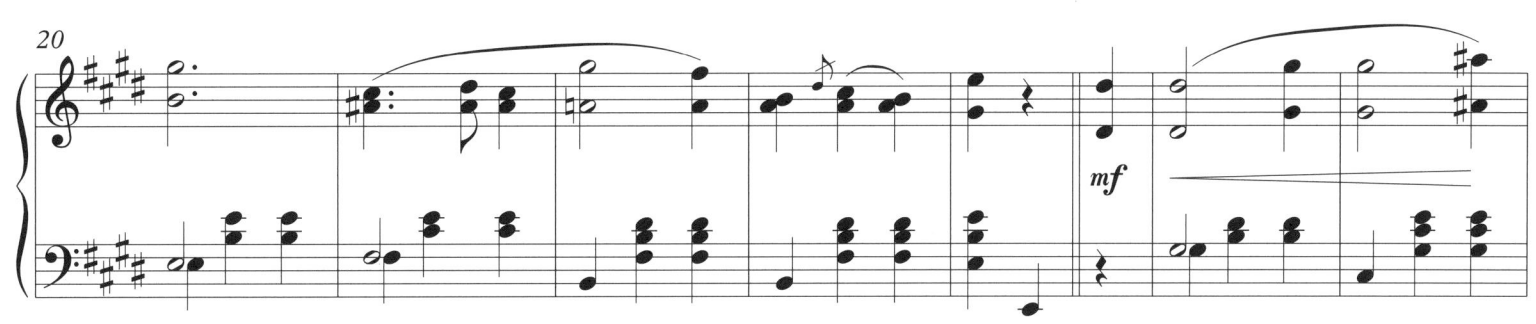
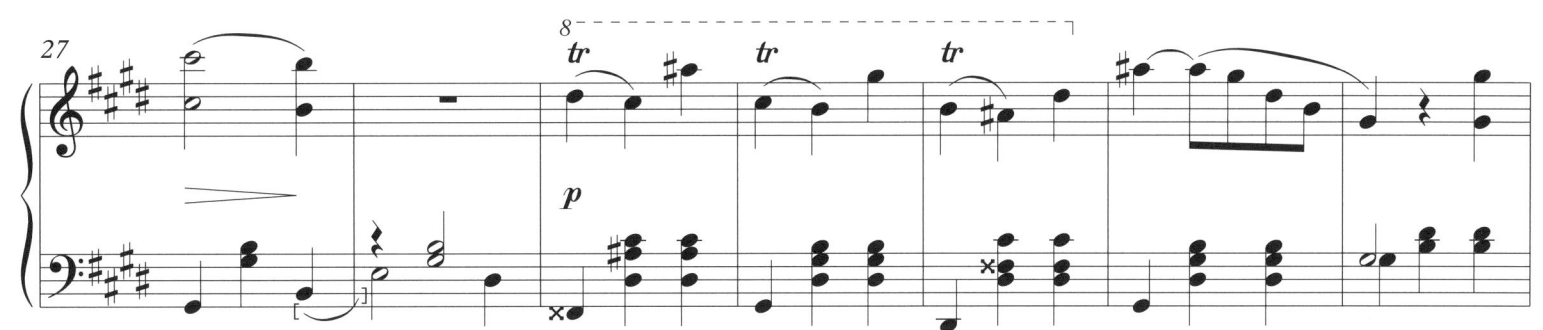

Valse

(Version based on **A**; see source information, p.135)

(Composed 1830)

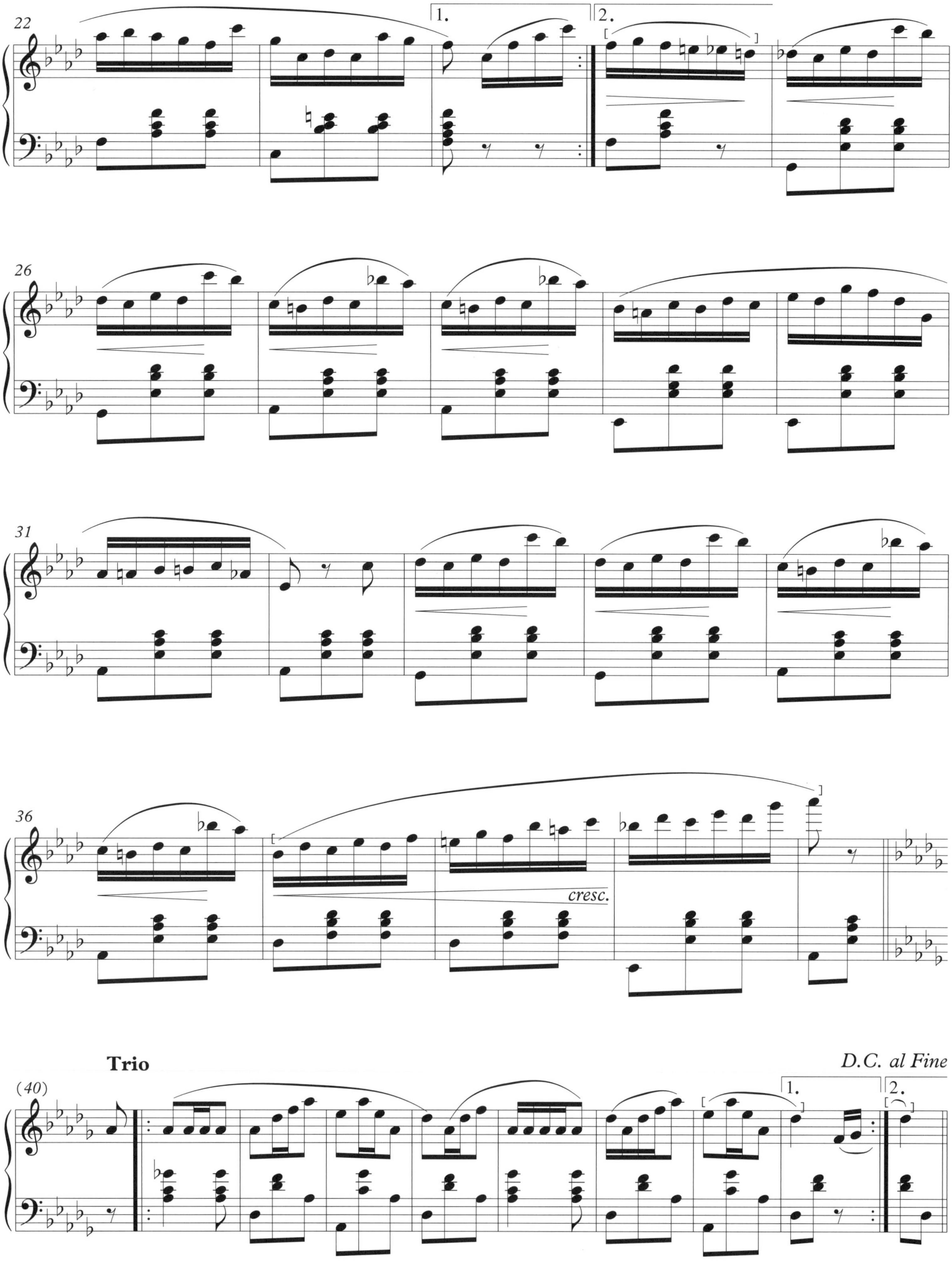
22
1.
2.
26
31
36
cresc.
Trio
D.C. al Fine
(40)
1.
2.

Valse

(Version based on **G**; see source information, p.135)

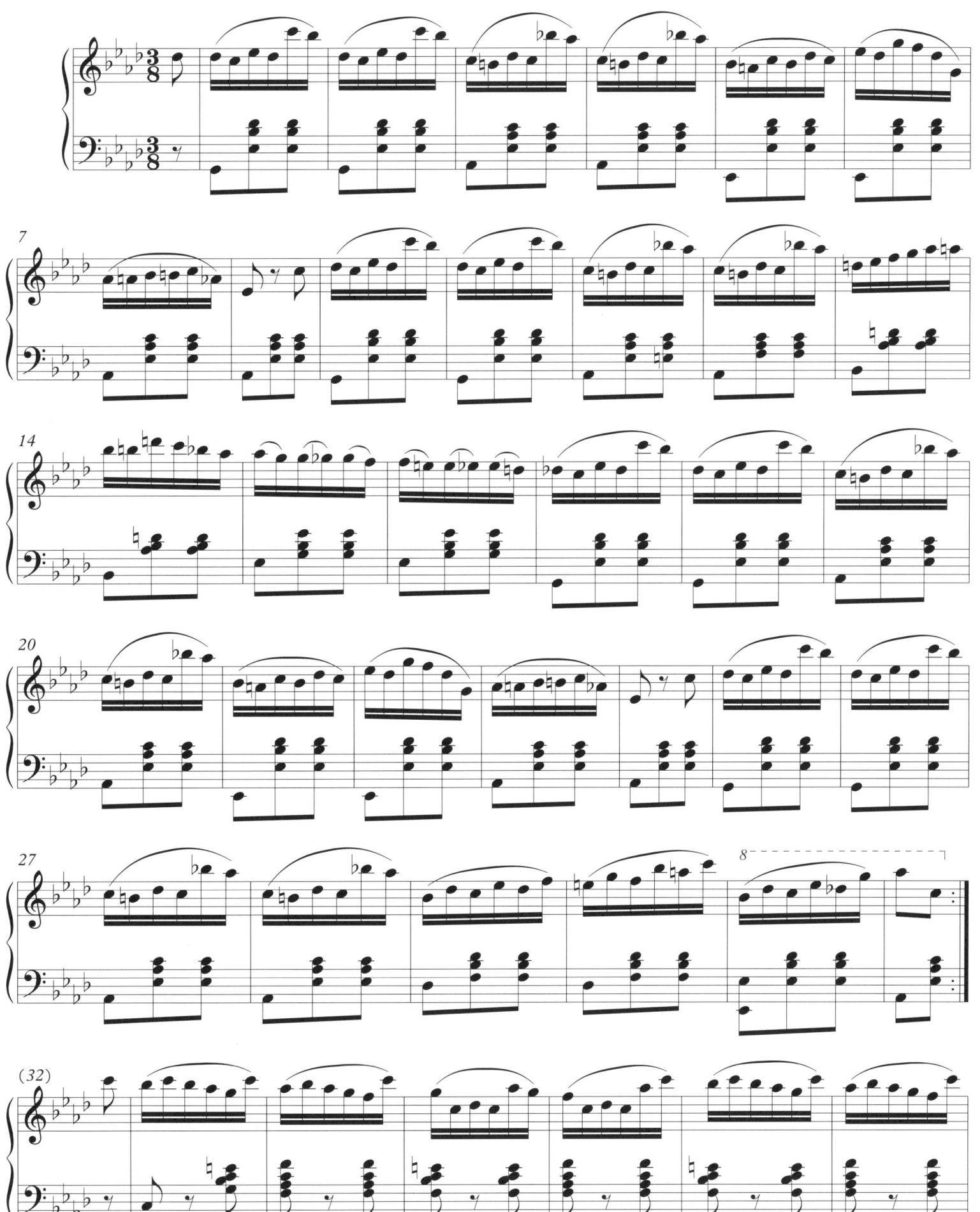

Valse

(Composed 1830)

Valse

(Version based on **A¹**; see source information, p.136)

(Composed 1832)

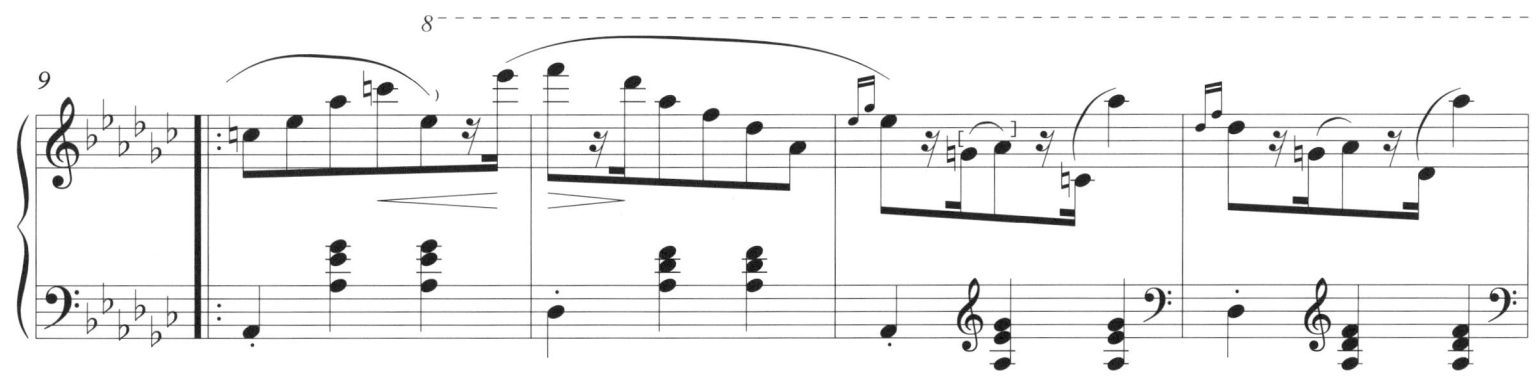

Valse

(Version based on **A²**; see source information, p.136)

Valse
pour Mlle Marie

(Version based on **A¹**; see source information, p.136)

(Composed 1835)

★ See Critical Commentary.

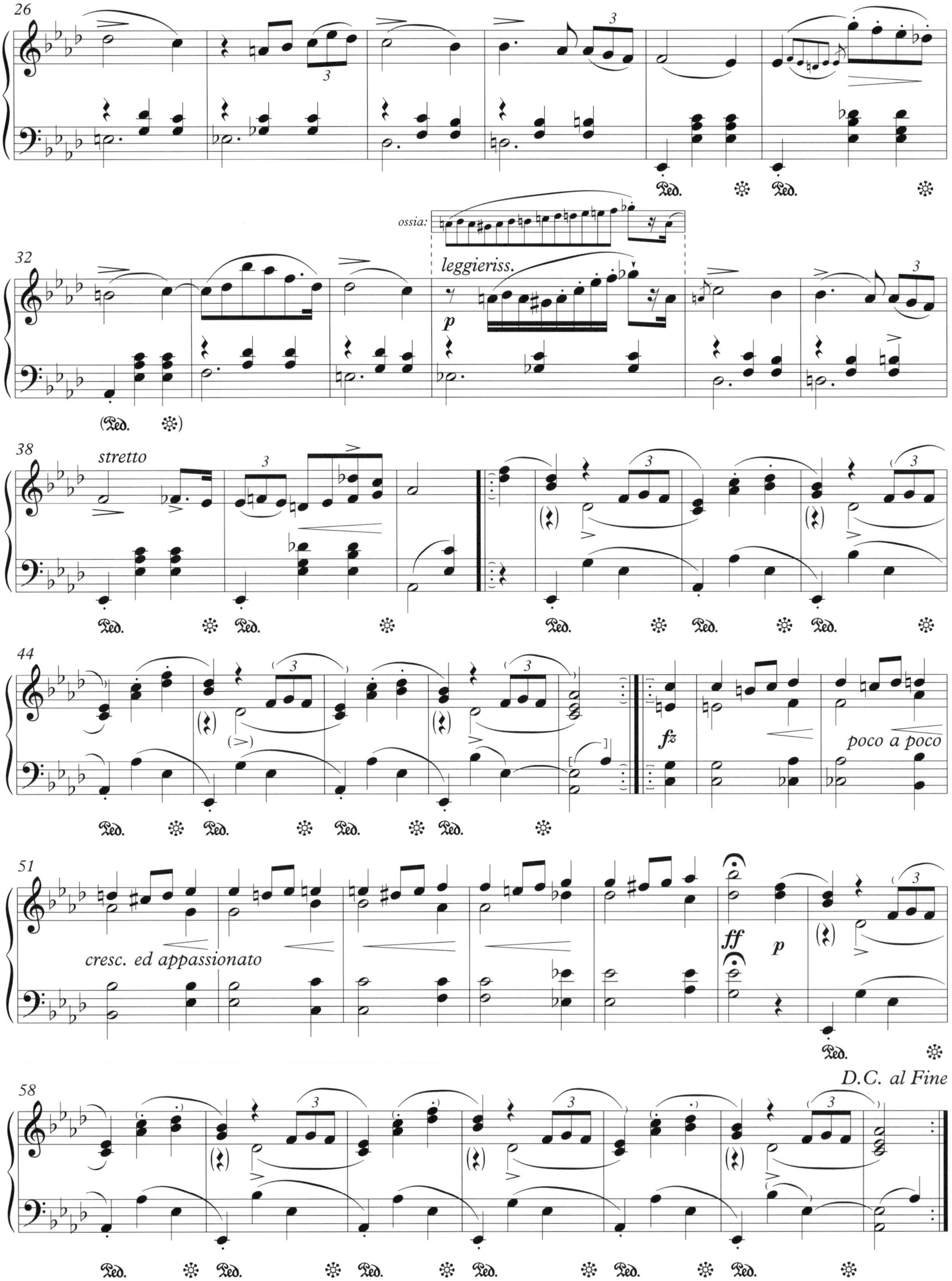
26
32
ossia:
leggieriss.
p
38
stretto
44
fz
poco a poco
51
cresc. ed appassionato
ff
p
D.C. al Fine
58

Valse

(Version based on **A³** with variants; see source information, pp.136–137)

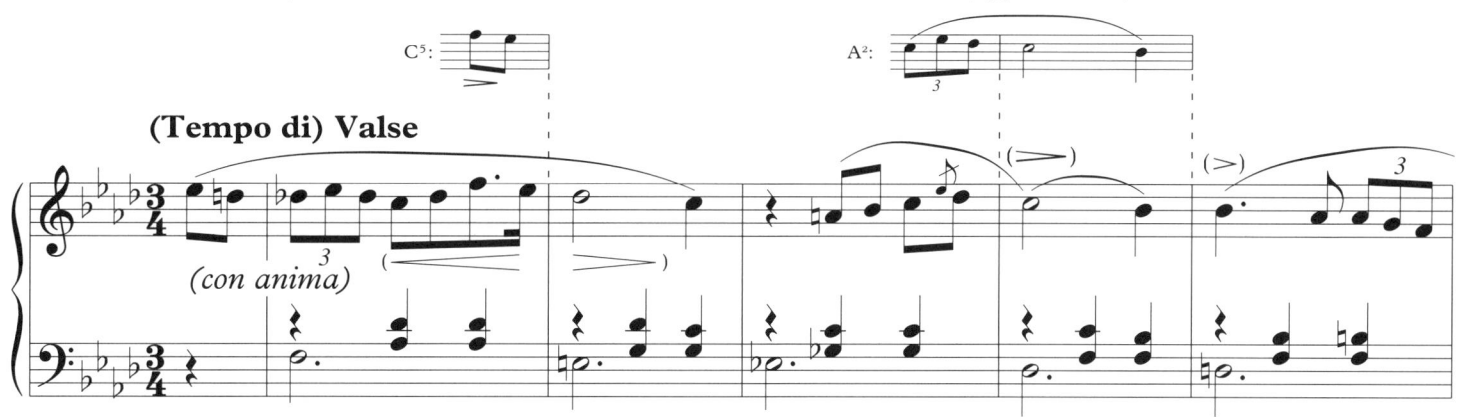
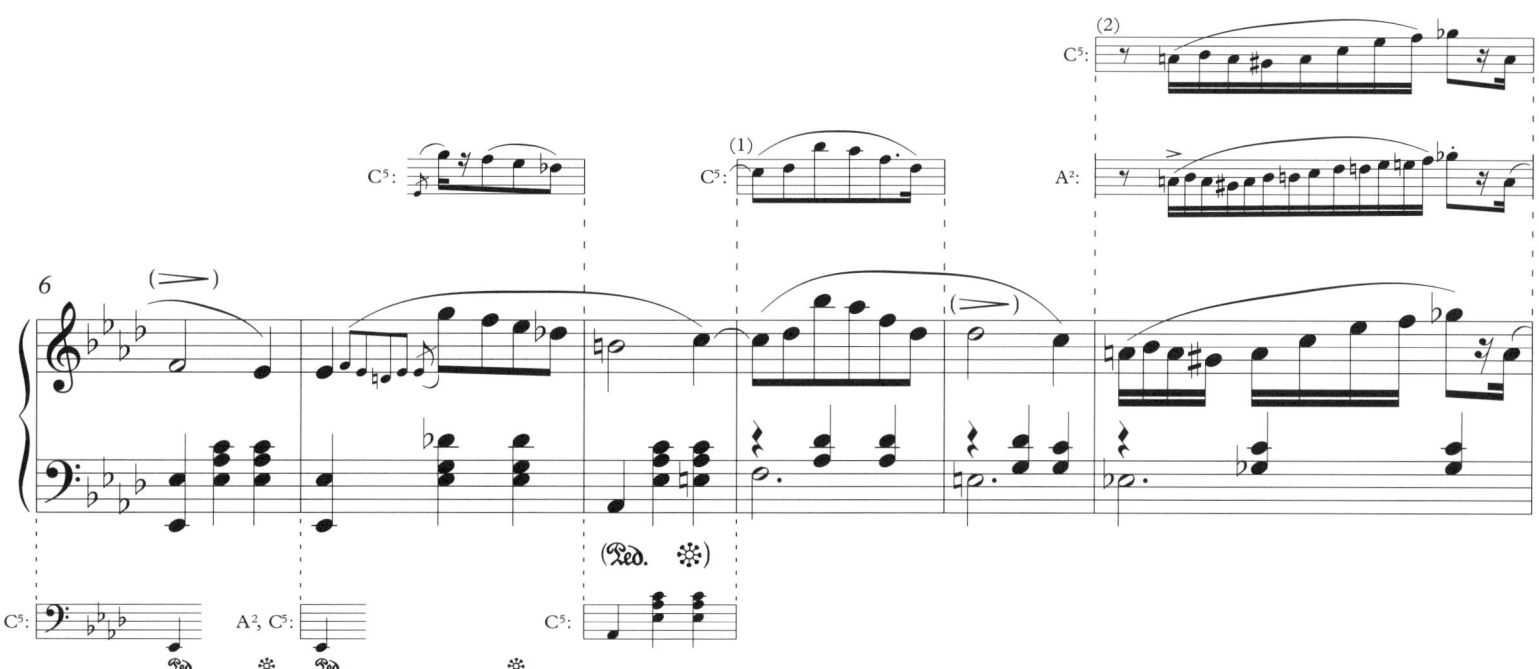

★ See Critical Commentary.

Valse

à Mlle Elise Gavard

(Version based on **A³**; see source information, p.137)

(Composed 1842)

Valse

(Version based on **P**; see source information, p.138)

Valse

Allegretto (Composed 1847)

APPENDIX

Valse, Op. 18

(Version based on **A¹**; see source information, p.125)

Valse, Op. 18

(Version based on **A²**; see source information, p.125)

Valse, Op. 34 No. 1

(Version based on **A**¹; see source information, p.126)

Tempo di Valse

★ See Critical Commentary.

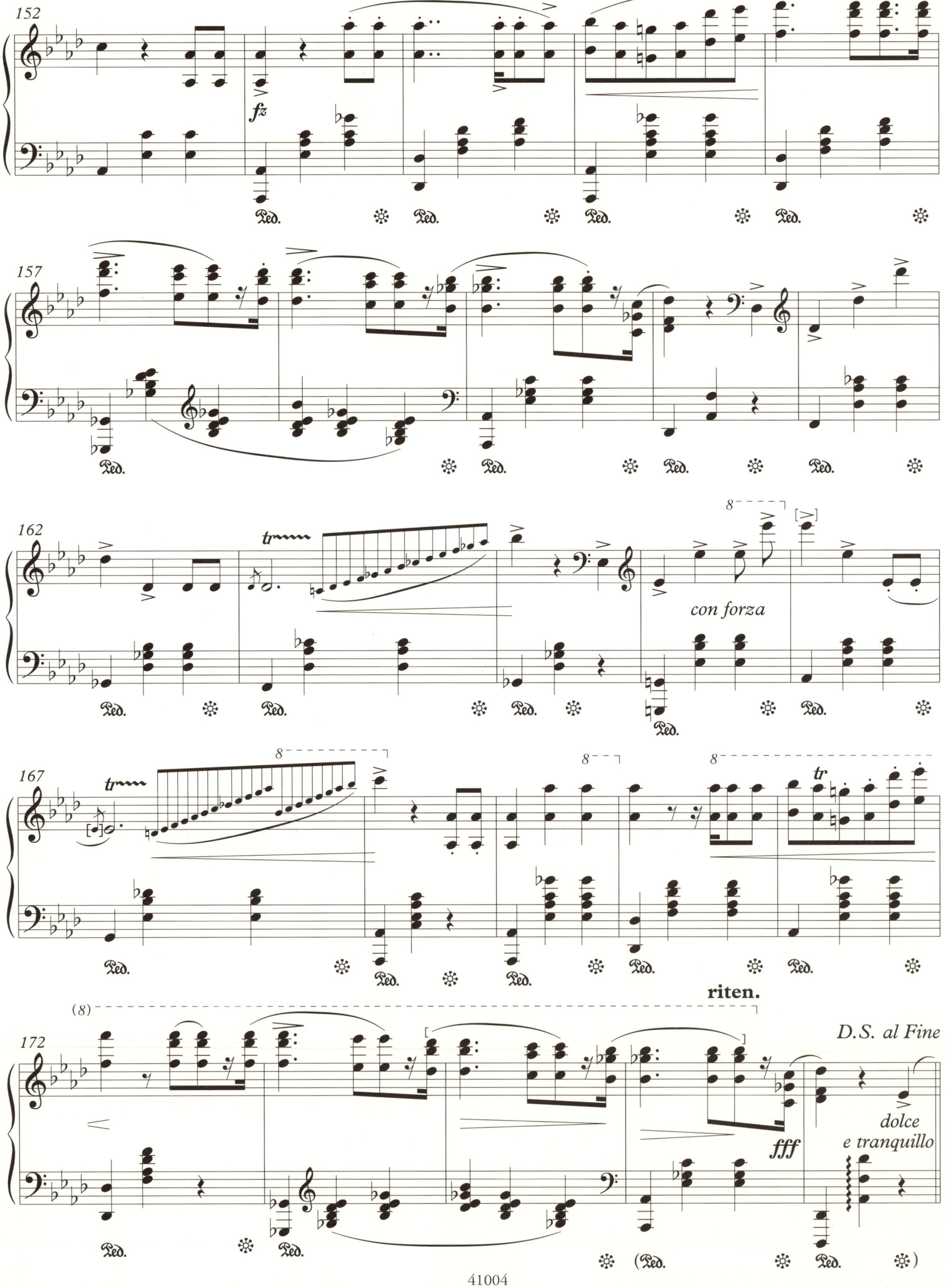

152
fz
Ped.
157
162
tr
8
con forza
167
tr
8
172
(8)
riten.
D.S. al Fine
fff
dolce
e tranquillo

Valse, Op. 64 No. 1

(Version based on **A³** with variants;
see source information, p.131)

★ In **A⁴,⁵** the sign 𝄋 is situated at the beginning of this bar, because of the difference in distribution of the music text which terminates in these sources at the end of bar 76.

★ See note p. 115.

Valse, Op. 64 No. 2

(Version based on **A²**; see source information, p.132)

NOTES ON EDITORIAL METHOD AND PRACTICE

Editorial concept

The Complete Chopin is based on two key premises. First, there can be no definitive version of Chopin's works: variants form an integral part of the music. Second, a permissive conflation of readings from several sources – in effect producing a version of the music that never really existed – should be avoided. Accordingly, our procedure is to identify a single principal source for each work and to prepare an edition of that source (which we regard as 'best', even if it cannot be definitive). At the same time, we reproduce important variants from other authorized sources either adjacent to or, in certain instances, within the main music text, in footnotes or in the Critical Commentary, thus enabling scholarly comparison and facilitating choice in performance. (Conflation may be inadmissible for the editor, but it remains an option and right for the performer.) Multiple versions of whole works are presented when differences between the sources are so abundant or fundamental that they go beyond the category of 'variant'.

Sources

The complexity of the Chopin sources could hardly be greater, given the varying ways in which each work was drafted, prepared for publication (usually in three different countries) and subsequently revised in successive impressions. Our edition takes account of the following sources as relevant:
- autograph manuscripts, many of which were used by engravers (i.e. *Stichvorlagen*, or engraver's manuscripts);
- proofs, whether uncorrected or corrected by Chopin;
- first editions, including subsequent impressions released during Chopin's lifetime if relevant;
- autograph glosses in the scores of his students and associates; and
- editions of pieces for which no other source material survives.

In determining a single principal source for each piece, we have been guided by several factors of variable relevance from work to work. For the music published during Chopin's lifetime, these include the following:
- Chopin's presence in Paris, which allowed him to correct proofsheets and successive impressions of the French first edition, whereas he had less control over the publication process in Germany and England. We therefore tend to privilege the French first edition and later printings thereof;
- the existence of an autograph or authoritative copy related to a particular first edition; and
- the quality of the source with respect to errors and clarity of presentation.

For the posthumously published works, a more *ad hoc* methodology must be adopted, taking into account extant autograph manuscripts or approved copies or early editions when no other source material survives. The rationale for the selection of each work's principal source is given in the Critical Commentary.

Editorial principles

Our central aim is fidelity to the designated principal source except when errors and omissions occur therein. When such errors and omissions are indisputable, corrections are made tacitly in the music text, without distinguishing marks, but are discussed in the Critical Commentary (except for certain types of accidental; see below). When they are open to debate, any changes made editorially are distinguished in the music text by the use of square brackets; the Critical Commentary will discuss and justify these changes as necessary.

When other authorized sources offer significant alternatives, we present these as variants in one of the following ways:

- *alternative music text* is positioned on the page, either next to the main text or in footnotes; the provenance of each variant is identified according to the system of abbreviations defined in the Critical Commentary;
- *alternative dynamics, articulation and other small-scale variants* are incorporated within the music text but are distinguished by round brackets;
- *alternative fingerings* are printed in italics; and
- *alternative pedallings* appear below the staff in smaller type and enclosed within round brackets, their provenance being identified according to the system of abbreviations defined in the Critical Commentary.

Minor alternatives in other authorized sources are discussed and reproduced in the Critical Commentary as necessary, but do not appear in the body of the edition proper.

The principle of fidelity to an early nineteenth-century source raises important questions about the appearance of our Edition, given the differences in notational conventions between Chopin's age and our own. Our general practice is to conserve relevant features of early to mid nineteenth-century notation while modernizing details which otherwise would not be comprehensible to today's performers. The criterion is whether or not a given feature has any bearing on the music's meaning. For instance, we generally follow the original notation with regard to the position of slurs before or after tied notes; the chains of small-scale slurs in Chopin's original texts; superimposed (multiple) slurs; unbroken beamings across multiple groups of quavers, semiquavers etc.; and the disposition of the hands across the staves. We also respect the expressive idiosyncrasies of parallel passages.

Select characteristics of the Edition

- *Square brackets* distinguish all editorial interventions except precautionary accidentals (which are added only when reading accuracy is jeopardized). *Round brackets* (parentheses) designate additions and variants from other authorized sources.
- *Accidentals* missing from the original source are tacitly replaced in this Edition when these are found within the same bar at a higher or lower register, and when they clearly apply to other uses of the same pitch class in that bar (this sort of omission being extremely typical of Chopin).
- No editorial *fingerings* have been added. When Chopin's own fingerings appear in the principal source, they are presented in roman type in our Edition. Any significant fingerings from other authorized sources appear in italics; their provenance is identified in the Critical Commentary.
- *Right- and left-hand parts* may be divided between the two staves when such a disposition is vital to the original sense or better conforms to hand positions. This is how Chopin tended to notate his music, and it may be significant with regard to articulation and sonority.
- *Accents* pose a major problem in Chopin editing. Accents of various sizes are found throughout Chopin's manuscripts (as well as many scribal copies) and apparently have different meanings according to context; nevertheless, such meanings can be difficult to ascertain, not least because of notational inconsistencies on Chopin's part which make the editor's job all the more vexed. This Edition preserves the two principal types of accent in Chopin's autographs: conventional accents (>) and 'long accents' (⇀). The latter seem to have various functions: to indicate dynamic reinforcement, expressive stress and proportional prolongation for notes of long rhythmic value (i.e. minims and semibreves); to convey a sense

of 'leaning' to appoggiaturas, suspensions and syncopations; to emphasize groups of two, three or four notes, as well as rolled chords; and to prolong a stress over tied notes. Long accents are best thought of as a 'surge', versus the dynamic retraction implied by a visually similar diminuendo sign (with which many early and modern Chopin editions alike replace the long accents intended by Chopin). Marcato accents (^, as opposed to >) are retained from the original.

- This Edition presents both *grace notes* (with stroke) and *'long appoggiaturas'* (without stroke), thus preserving a distinction clearly intended by Chopin.
- A flexible approach to *stem directions* on a single staff has been taken. Standard modern practice is not observed when the original stem directions convey a meaning that modernized notation would lack.
- *Liaisons* (i.e. diagonal lines) between the hands are reproduced where relevant; taken from the copies of Chopin's students (especially those of Camille Dubois), these indicate a simultaneous attack on the beat with both hands.
- *Rests* are added only when the original sense is unclear or in cases of error or omission.
- *Pedalling.* Where a 𝒫𝑒𝑑. marking or pedal release (✳) is either erroneous or absent, and when its placement is unambiguous, such an indication is inserted without square brackets but is discussed in the Critical Commentary; when its placement is open to debate, any editorial correction or addition will be designated by square brackets, with justification provided in the Critical Commentary as necessary. In general, pedal releases are not added at the ends of pieces: the pedalling remains 'open' in keeping with Chopin's practice.
- *Triplets* and similar rhythmic groupings are indicated with small numbers. Such groupings and similar ornamental shapes are not slurred as a matter of policy, as such slurs in Chopin's music often designate legato articulation, not rhythmic grouping. We therefore follow his notational practice.
- Elements in the principal source deemed to be superfluous (e.g. redundant accidentals, pedal releases, slurs, and staccato or augmentation dots) are not retained in this Edition; the Critical Commentary will discuss only those elements which are open to debate.

Critical Commentary

The Critical Commentary identifies the particular strategy for the choice of primary and secondary sources, provides information on sources (including dates and library sigla as necessary) and justifies individual decisions regarding the text. It also reports on relevant variants and corrections of errors and omissions in the principal source. The identification of obvious mistakes and faulty notation in the sources is avoided; so too is the description of secondary musical details in subsidiary sources.

Standard library sigla are given as relevant for manuscript material. The following abbreviations are used when necessary:

RH = right hand
LH = left hand
Br. = brass
Str. = strings
Ww. = woodwind; plus standard abbreviations for other orchestral instruments.

To specify pitches, the Helmholtz system is used as follows:

C_2 C_1 C   c c^1 c^2 c^3 c^4

An oblique (/) is used for comments applying to more than one part (e.g. 'RH/LH' refers to both RH and LH). Commas are used in succession when a given feature occurs in a number of bars or sources (e.g. 'Bars 6, 7, 8. > to RH note 2 from **F**') or when a given element has multiple features (e.g. 'Bar 19. *p*, > to LH chord 1 from **S**').

This Edition employs a precise and unambiguous means of identifying individual notes and chords within a bar. In general, these are referred to in the Critical Commentary with regard to their position as an *event* within a given bar. For instance, in the following music example (the first bar from the E minor Concerto Op. 11):

'w' = bar 1 RH note 3, as it is a single note and the third right-hand event in the bar;
'x' = bar 1 RH chord 4, as it is a chord (i.e. two or more notes) and the fourth right-hand event in the bar;
'y' = bar 1 LH note 2, as it is a single note and the second left-hand event in the bar; and
'z' = bar 1 LH chord 3, as it is a chord (i.e. two or more notes) and the third left-hand event in the bar.

Acknowledgements

Financial support for *The Complete Chopin* has been generously provided by the Arts and Humanities Research Council, the British Academy, the British Council, the Swiss National Science Foundation, and the Department of Music, Royal Holloway, University of London.

John Rink
Jim Samson
Jean-Jacques Eigeldinger
Christophe Grabowski

CRITICAL COMMENTARY

WALTZ OP. 18

Sources

A¹	Autograph, dated 10 July 1833. [US-NYpm: Lehman deposit]
A²	Autograph, more developed than **A¹**, 1833. [Pl-Wtfc: M/2308]
A³	Autograph, May 1834.* *Stichvorlage* for **F¹**. [B-MA: 1093/4]
[**FP**]	Hypothetical proofs of **F¹**. *Stichvorlagen* for **G¹** and **E¹**.
F¹	French first edition, June 1834. M. Schlesinger, Paris, plate no. M.S. 1599.
F²	Corrected reprint of **F¹**, 1834.
F³	Reprint of **F²**, 1842. Henry Lemoine, Paris, plate no. HL 2777.
F = **F¹⁻³**	
G¹	German first edition, July 1834. Breitkopf & Härtel, Leipzig, plate no. 5545.
G²	German second edition (publisher and plate no. as for **G¹**), ca 1840.
G = **G¹,²**	
E¹	English first edition. Wessel & Co., London, plate no. W & Cº Nº 1157, August 1834.
E²	Corrected reprint of **E¹**, 1839.
E = **E¹,²**	
D¹	Dubois copy of **F²**. [F-Pn: Rés. F. 980 (IV)]
D²	Dubois copy of **F³**. [F-Pn: Rés. F. 980 (III)]
S	Stirling copy of **F²**. [F-Pn: Rés. Vma 241 (II, 18)]
J	Jędrzejewicz copy of **F³**. [PL-Wtfc: M/175]

Suggested filiation

In **A¹** and **A²**, this Waltz is in a simple *da capo* form. The definitive version, **A³**, served as the basis of **F¹**; uncorrected proofs of **F¹** were used to prepare **G¹** and **E¹**. Apart from the articulation, **G¹** remains faithful to its source. By contrast, **E¹** and especially **E²** contain supplementary dynamic indications and other corrections originating from the revisions effected in London. The corrections in **F²** are in all likelihood Chopin's.

The principal source for this edition is **F²**, which was the final source corrected by the composer. Versions based on **A¹** and **A²**, which differ considerably from the published text, are given in the Appendix.

Version based on F²

It is difficult to distinguish between long and short accents in **F**. To ensure maximum clarity, the accent sizes have been more clearly differentiated in this edition. The articulation is inconsistent in all the sources, particularly staccato dots and wedges. As far as possible, the articulation here is from **F²**; markings from **A³** (enclosed in parentheses) or given by analogy [within square brackets] are not referred to in the Critical Commentary. However, all editorial interventions which modify the articulation of the principal source are enclosed in square brackets in the musical text and discussed in the Critical Commentary. Unless indicated otherwise, all fingering is from **D¹**.

Bar 1.	**E**: *p*
Bar 5.	*f* from **A³**
Bars 8, 16.	> to LH note 3 from **A³**
Bars 8, 40.	Staccato dots to RH chords 2, 3 from **A²**
Bars 12–13, 44–45, 165–166, 166–168, 169–170.	**D¹** contains LH slurs over barline from LH note 1 to first LH note in next bar; these suggest that the dotted minims provide the harmonic foundation and should be fully sustained
Bar 19.	**F**, **G**, **E**: RH slur ends RH note 5 (cf. **A³**)
Bars 19–20b.	RH slur over barline by analogy with bars 19–20a
Bar 20a.	Fingering from **J**
Bar 20b.	Upper fingering to RH note 2 from **J**; its logical continuation (3, 2, 1) is an alternative to fingering in **D¹**.
Bars 21, 25.	Identical fingering to RH notes 1, 4 in **J**
Bar 34.	Identical fingering to RH note 1 in **J**
Bar 35.	No pedalling in any source; here as in bar 27
Bars 40, 48.	> to LH note 3 from **A²**
Bar 42.	Long accent from **A³**
Bar 48.	> to RH note 3 as in bar 16
Bar 51.	> to RH note 1 from **A²**
Bar 58.	**F**, **G**, **E**: single slur to RH notes 1–6, attributable to French engraver's misreading of Chopin's notation; here as in bars 26, 34 *et seq.*
Bar 69.	**A¹⁻³**, **E²**: *dolce* (cf. comment to bar 99)
Bar 71.	Identical fingering to RH chord 1 in **S**
Bars 72, 106, 110.	**F**: staccato wedge to RH note 1; here staccato dot by analogy with bar 70
Bar 75.	Identical fingering to RH chords 2, 3 in **S**
Bar 76.	Identical fingering to $d\flat^2$ RH chord 1 in **S**
Bars 76, 77, 78, 79, 80.	LH slur by analogy with bars 69, 70, 71, 72, 73, 74
Bars 81, 113.	**A²,³**, **F**, **G**, **E**: RH chord 4 has only a downward stem; upward stem added here to $g\flat^2$ to clarify counterpoint and by analogy with bars 82, 114
Bars 81–82.	RH slur over barline from **A³**
Bar 84a.	No slur from bar 84a RH note 4 to bar 69 RH note 1 in any source; here by analogy with bars 68–69, 106–107
Bars 83–84b.	RH slur over barline by analogy with bars 83–84a
Bar 84b.	> to RH chord 2 from **A³**
Bar 88.	LH chord 4: upward stem by analogy with bar 96
Bar 95.	> to RH note 5 and pedalling as in bar 87
Bar 96.	LH chord 4: upward stem from **A²**
Bar 99.	**A³**: *dolcissimo*, not *dolce*; no marking in **G**, **E**. Fingering from **D²**.
Bar 100.	Fingering to RH note 4 from **D²**
Bars 101–102.	**F**, **E**: RH slur ends bar 101 chord 2; here as in bars 69–70
Bars 101–114.	LH slurs by analogy with bars 69–76
Bar 106.	> to RH note 4 from **A³**
Bars 112–113.	RH slur over barline from **A²**
Bars 113, 114.	> to RH chord 4 from **A³**
Bars 126–128.	**A³**, **F**, **G**: no ✽ to bar 126 LH chord 3, no pedalling bars 127–128; pedalling here as in bars 158–160
Bar 127.	**F**: staccato wedge to RH note 1; here staccato dot by analogy with bars 151, 159
Bars 131–132a/b.	RH slur over barline by analogy with bars 129–130, 130–131

---

* See letter from A. Franchomme to J. Forest dated 11 May 1834 in Sophie Ruhlmann, 'Chopin - Franchomme', *op. cit.*, p. 121.

Bar 135.	**F**: staccato wedge to RH note 2; staccato dot here seems more suited to musical context. Staccato dots to RH notes 4, 6 from **A²**.
Bar 136.	Staccato dots to RH notes 2, 4, 6 from **A²**
Bar 145.	Accent to RH note 2 from **A²**
Bar 157.	Fingering from **J**
Bars 163–164b.	Slur over barline by analogy with bars 163–164a
Bar 164a.	No slur from bar 164a RH note 2 to bar 133 RH note 1 in any source; here by analogy with bars 132b–133
Bars 167, 171.	*p* from **D¹**
Bars 168–170.	**D¹**: one continuous RH slur from bar 168 RH note 3 to bar 170 RH note 2, marked as correction (see also bars 153–154 of version based on **A¹** in Appendix)
Bars 176–177.	**F, G, E**: RH slur over barline incorrectly ends bar 176 RH note 5
Bar 178.	**A³, F¹, G, E**: no ♮ to g♭ LH chord 2
Bars 179–180.	**D¹**: numeral '2' marked above RH staff, at beginning of bar, in this musical context indicating use of *una corda* pedal
Bar 181.	Ped. from **A³**, which lacks corresponding ✽ on beat 3. Pianists may wish to use pedal from bar 183 beat 1 to bar 185 beat 2.
Bar 194.	Accent by analogy with bar 193
Bar 195.	Pedalling as in bar 11
Bars 203–204.	RH slur over barline from **A³**
Bar 221.	**A³, F**: staccato wedge to RH note 1; here staccato dot by analogy with bars 222, 223
Bars 229, 230.	Accent to LH note 1 from **D¹**
Bar 231.	**A³, F, G, E**: *f¹*, not *d¹*, to LH chords 2, 3; here as in bars 191, 198, where Chopin improved the harmony
Bars 245–248.	Pedalling from **A³**
Bars 249–250.	Pedalling by analogy with bars 244–245 in **A³**
Bar 261.	*fz* from **A³**
Bar 263.	Ped. from **A³**, which lacks corresponding ✽. This pedalling is recommended for the analogous bars that follow.
Bar 267.	Slur to lower RH voice by analogy with bar 268
Bar 268.	*fz* from **A³**
Bar 269.	In all editions, slur to lower RH voice spans RH notes 1–4, probably reflecting interventions by French engraver which escaped Chopin's attention when correcting the proofs. Here as in **A³**; cf. also slurring of similar motifs. *fz*, ⸺ by analogy with bar 268.
Bar 271.	Accent from **A³**
Bars 273–274, 277–278, 279.	Upper RH fingering from **J**; its logical continuation (2, 1, 3, 2 in bars 273, 277, 279; 4, 3, 2, 1 in bars 274, 278) is an alternative to **D¹**'s fingering
Bars 277, 278.	**G, E**: erroneous ♭ to *c²* RH chord/note 1 originates from **[FP]**
Bar 279.	**G, E**: erroneous ♭ to *d¹* in RH chord 1 originates from **[FP]**
Bar 280.	> to RH note 1 from **A³**; fingering from **J**
Bar 281.	> to RH note 1 from **A³**. **A³, F, G**: RH slur extends to RH note 4, not note 5; here by analogy with bars 278, 280 (see also **E**)
Bar 282.	> by analogy with bar 280; RH slur, staccato dot to RH note 5 from **G**
Bar 283.	Accent to RH note 1 from **D¹**
Bar 287.	**D²**: Ped. is indicated by large letters above RH staff; this may be to encourage prompt depression of pedal in order to sustain first note in bar. Alternatively, and more significantly, the marking could prescribe subtle use of pedal throughout final part of coda.
Bars 287–288.	⸺ from **D¹**. **A³**: broken *crescendo* line starting in bar 288 suggests radical dynamic change on RH beat 2 of bar 287; prevailing *p* (added here editorially) seems to have been forgotten by Chopin
Bar 295.	Fingering from **J**
Bars 295, 297, 297, 298, 299, 300, 301, 302, 303.	All editions incorrectly end RH slur at RH note 5, instead of continuing over barline (cf. **A³** bars 295–296)
Bar 304.	Omitted in **A³, G, E**

WALTZ OP. 34 NO. 1

Sources

A¹	Autograph, bearing indication 'Tempo di Valse', dedicated 'à Mlle la C^sse J. de Thun' and dated 'Tetschen le 15 Sept. 1835'; lost, but reproduced in *Kwartalnik muzyczny*, 1949.
A²	Autograph. *Stichvorlage* for **F**. [PL-Wtm 7/Ch.]
[FP]	Hypothetical proofs of **F¹**. *Stichvorlage* for **G**.
F¹	French first edition, first impression published within *Album des Pianistes* […] *10ᵉ Année*, 1st December 1838. M. Schlesinger, Paris, plate no. M.S. 2715.1.
F²	Corrected reprint of **F¹**, December 1838.
F = F¹·²	
G	German first edition, December 1838. Breitkopf & Härtel, Leipzig, plate no. 6032.
E	English first edition, December 1838. Wessel & Co., London, plate no. W & Cº Nº 2280.
D	Dubois copy of **F²**. [F-Pn: Rés.F.980 (III, 5/1)]
S	Stirling copy of **F²**. [F-Pn: Rés. Vma 241 (IV, 34/I)]

Suggested filiation

Although **F** was based on **A²**, there are discrepancies between these sources, above all in the pedalling (which is sparse in **A²**). Prior to departing for Majorca, Chopin apparently asked Fontana to correct the French proofs; it is therefore likely that most of the changes introduced into **F** were Fontana's. The proofs of **F¹** were sent to Leipzig and served as the basis of **G**. **E**, by contrast, was based on **F²**, which already contained most of the supplementary pedal markings, but which contained imperfections in the music text. The original title, marked by Chopin on the title page of **A²**, was 'Trois Valses pour piano oeuvre 34'. The French publisher altered this to 'Trois Grandes Valses brillantes'.

The principal source for this edition is **F²**. A version based on **A¹**, which differs considerably from the published text, is also given in the Appendix.

Version based on F²

Bars 1–2, 5–6, 9–16.	**A², F¹, G**: no pedalling

Bar 3.	Pedalling from **A²**. Staccato dots to LH beats 2, 3 from **G**, **E**.
Bar 4.	Staccato dots to LH beats 1, 2 from **G**, **E**
Bar 7.	**F**, **G**: ✻ positioned after beat 3; here as in **A²**, **E**
Bar 11.	═══ by analogy with bars 10, 12
Bars 11, 12.	LH slur from **G**, **E**
Bar 12.	**F** has erroneous 𝄢 corrected to 𝄞 in **S**
Bars 17, 177.	**E**: *dolce* marked between staves
Bar 24.	**A²**, **F**, **G**, **E**: ℘ under LH note 1, lacking corresponding ✻; see also comment to bars 25–31
Bars 24, 32, 91, 184, 192, 272.	LH crotchet rest added to clarify counterpoint and by analogy with similar bars
Bars 25–31.	Pedalling from **A¹**, here altered slightly in bars 25–26 in accordance with harmonic context
Bars 33, 34, 36.	Fingering from **S**
Bars 39, 40.	Fingering from **S**, **D**
Bars 40, 48a/b, 200.	Staccato dot to RH chord 1 from **A²**
Bar 44.	Fingering from **S**
Bars 47–48b.	RH slur over barline by analogy with bars 47–48a
Bar 49.	**F**, **E**: no ♭ to *g* LH chord 2 (cf. **A²**, **G**, **S**)
Bar 54.	> to RH note 4 from **A²**
Bars 59–63, 75–79, 219–223, 235–238.	**A²**, **F**, **G**: no RH slurs or staccato dots; here as in bars 155–160; **E** has similar slurring but different articulation (wedge staccatos)
Bar 63.	**F**: RH chord 2 mistakenly engraved as a crotchet
Bar 65.	Accent from **A²**. Fingering from **D**.
Bar 67.	**F**: no ♭ to *g¹* LH chord 3
Bars 67, 227.	> to RH note 1 from **A²**
Bar 67–68.	**A²**, **F**, **G**: slur ends RH note 14; here by analogy with bar 72 (see also **E**)
Bars 67–68, 71–72.	Ascending scales inconsistently notated in all sources; notation here follows that of bars 71–72 in **A²**.
Bar 69.	**F**, **G**, **E**: erroneous *a*♭, not *b*♭, in LH chord 2 (cf. **A²**). Accent to RH note 2 by analogy with bar 165.
Bars 71, 231.	Accent to RH note 1 by analogy with bars 67, 167.
Bars 75–76.	═══ from **A¹** and as in bars 59–60
Bars 77, 78.	Fingering from **S**
Bars 81–82.	LH slur from **A²**
Bar 82.	Arpeggiando sign to RH beat 3 from **D**
Bars 83, 99, 131.	**F**, **G**, **E**: erroneous tie to LH notes 2, 3 (**A¹**: no tie; the crossing-out in **A²** here was interpreted by French engraver as tie)
Bars 84–88.	**F**, **G**, **E**: RH slur wrongly begins bar 85 RH chord 1, while in **F**, **E** it incorrectly ends bar 88 RH chord 2 (cf. **A¹,²**).
Bars 85–86, 101–102.	Complementary pedalling as in bars 133–134 (continuous pedalling ill-suited to modern piano)
Bar 87.	**A¹,²**: no pedalling; in all editions ✻ incorrectly situated after LH chord 3
Bar 89.	**F**, **G**, **E**: erroneous *gb¹*, not *ab¹*, in RH chord 4 (cf. **A²**)
Bar 91.	Slur to RH chords 2–3 from **A²**. Downward stem to LH note 3 from **A²** (cf. incorrect upward stem in **F**, **G**, **E**).
Bar 99.	**F**, **G**, **E**: RH slur begins RH chord 2; here as in bar 83
Bars 105, 137.	**F**, **G**, **E**: RH slur ends RH chord 4; here as in bar 90
Bar 106.	**F**, **G**, **E**: RH slur begins RH chord 1, not RH chord 2; here as in bar 91
Bars 107, 139.	**F**, **G**, **E**: slur to RH notes 1–3 (cf. **A²**)
Bars 111–112, 143–144.	Slur over barline from **A²**
Bar 112.	Upward stem added to RH note 2 to reflect its melodic function.
Bars 112–113, 117–118.	RH slur from **A²**
Bar 120.	*f* to RH note 2 from **A²**; see comment to bar 112 with regard to upward stem to RH note 2
Bar 138.	**F**, **G**: no slur; here as in bar 90
Bar 144.	**A²**: no pedalling. **F**, **G**, **E**: no ✻.
Bar 145.	**F**, **G**, **E**: ℘ incorrectly positioned under beat 2
Bar 157.	*ff* from **A²**
Bar 158.	Fingering from **S**
Bar 159.	Staccato dots to RH chords 1, 3 from **A²**
Bars 161, 162.	RH accent from **A²**
Bars 163–164.	**A²**, **F**, **G**: slur ends RH note 14, staccato dot (not wedge staccato) to RH note 15; here as in bars 71–72
Bars 163–164, 167–168.	**D** contains variants in form of added line suggesting extension of scales by one octave, as in bar 167 of version based on **A¹** (see Appendix). See also comment to bars 67–68, 71–72.
Bar 164.	**F**, **G**, **E**: ✻ immediately after beat 2; here by analogy with bar 168
Bar 165.	Staccato dot to RH note 1 from **A²**
Bar 166.	Accent to RH beat 3 by analogy with bar 162
Bars 167–168.	RH slur as in bars 71–72
Bar 171.	LH chord 2: erroneous *ab¹* in all printed sources; *gb¹* from **A²**
Bars 171–172.	RH slur over barline from **E** and by analogy with bars 155–156
Bar 173.	Slur to RH chords 2–3 from **A²**, **E**
Bar 175.	RH chord 4: *c¹* from **A²** (incorrectly omitted in **F**, **G**, **E**)
Bars 175–176.	RH slur over barline as in **A¹**
Bar 176.	**F**, **E**: ✻ after beat 3 (**G**: no ✻). *p* and '⌣' from **S**, where the latter appears as line crossing the bar, suggesting pause before main theme's reprise.
Bars 184–191.	See comment to bars 24–31
Bar 186.	**F**, **A²**, **G**: no ♭ to RH note 1; **F**, **A²**: no tie between RH grace note and RH minim *g¹*; here as in **E** and by analogy with bar 26
Bar 189.	**F**, **G**, **E**: no *eb¹* LH chord 2, 3; here as in bar 29
Bar 195.	**F**, **G**: change from bass clef to treble clef in LH mistakenly omitted before LH chord 2
Bars 207–208.	**F**, **G**: no pedalling; here as in **A²**, **E**
Bar 212.	**F**, **G**, **E**: ✻ positioned after beat 3; here as in bar 52
Bar 214.	> to RH note 4 from **A²**
Bar 225.	Accent to RH note 2 from **A²**
Bars 227–228.	**F**, **G**: slur ends RH note 14; here as in bars 71–72
Bars 227–228, 231–232.	Wedge staccato to RH note 15 from **A¹**. See also comment to bars 67–68, 71–72.
Bar 229.	Accent to RH beat 2 by analogy with bar 165

Bars 235–236.
> ─── from **E** and by analogy with bars 219–220

Bars 238–239.
> RH slur over barline by analogy with **A²** bars 242–243

Bars 239–240, 243–244.
> Tie to RH f^2s over barline from **A²**

Bars 241–242.
> RH slur over barline from **E** and by analogy with bars 158–159

Bars 242–243.
> RH slur over barline from **A²**

Bars 245, 258, 262, 266.
> Fingering from **S**

Bars 248, 249, 250.
> > from **A²**

Bars 251, 252.
> > by analogy with bars 248–250

Bars 252–253.
> **F, G, E**: RH slur ends bar 252 RH note 6 (cf. **A²**)

Bar 253. Staccato dot to RH note 1 from **A²**
Bar 257. Pedalling by analogy with bars 253 *et seq.*
Bars 268–269.
> LH slur over barline from **A²**

Bars 272–273.
> Tie to LH fs over barline from **A²**

Bars 276–277.
> **F, G, E**: RH slur ends bar 276 RH note 6; in **A²** slur extends beyond bar line, suggesting its prolongation until bar 277 RH note 1

Bar 280. Staccato dot from **A²**
Bar 286. LH note 1: $A\flat$ from **A²** (**F, G, E**: incorrect $E\flat$)
Bar 293. Long accent from **A²**
Bar 299. **F, G, E**: ✱ positioned after bar 298 beat 3; here as in bar 297

WALTZ OP. 34 NO. 2

Sources

A Working autograph. *Stichvorlage* for **F**. [photograph, Archiwum Akt Nowych, Warsaw, Poland]

F French first edition, published both separately and within *Album des Pianistes* […] *10ᵉ Année*, 1st December 1838. M. Schlesinger, Paris, plate no. M.S. 2716.2.

G German first edition, December 1838. Breitkopf & Härtel, Leipzig, plate no. 6033.

E English first edition, December 1838. Wessel & Co., London, plate no. W & Cᵒ Nᵒ 2281.

D Dubois copy of **F**. [F-Pn: Rés.F.980 (III, 5/2)]

J Jędrzejewicz copy of **F**. [Pl-Wtfc: M/175]

S Stirling copy of **F**. [F-Pn: Rés. Vma 241 (IV, 34/II)]

Suggested filiation

A was the *Stichvorlage* for **F**, which served as the basis of **G** and **E**. As with Op. 34 No. 1, it is likely that Fontana corrected the Parisian proofs of this work. The title 'Grande Valse brillante', found in all the original editions despite the work's melancholy character, was added by the French publisher.

The principal source for this edition is **A**. All fingering is from **S**, unless indicated otherwise.

Bars 8, 160, 196.
> **D, J, S**: almost certainly Chopin's definitive version rather than a variant. **D**: no $g\sharp^1$ in RH chord 1.

Bars 8, 57, 59, 73 *et seq.*
> LH crotchet rest added to clarify counterpoint

Bars 17, 19. **F, G**: no RH slurs
Bars 17–20. **A** contains many corrections to RH slurring. Discernible through the deletions, the original RH version was as follows:

Bar 18. **A**: no ♯ to RH note 2
Bars 22, 23, 90, 91.
> **A**: no augmentation dot to LH note 1

Bars 23, 91. Tie to LH *a*s beats 2, 3 from **F, G, E**
Bars 24, 92. ∿ from **F, G, E**
Bars 32, 100. **A**: RH notes 2–4 incorrectly notated as triplet quavers

Bars 40, 42, 44, 45, 48, 50 *et seq.*
> Staccato dot to LH note 1 by analogy with bars 37, 38, 39

Bars 45, 113. LH slur as in bar 37
Bars 46–50. Indicated in **A** as repeat of bars 38–43
Bars 53, 121. f from **F, G, E**
Bar 67. RH notes 2, 3: fingering in **J** accords with **S**. Fingering to RH note 6 from **D**.
Bar 68. Fingering from **D**
Bars 68, 136. **A**: no ♮ to RH note 2. The original pedalling does not allow *A* LH note 1 to be sustained. Editorial solution proposed in music text allows sustaining of this note without use of pedal. Alternatively, new pedal may be applied from beat 1 to end beat 2.

Bars 69, 137. p from **F, E**
Bars 81, 149. ℘. from **F, E**
Bars 81. Lower RH fingering to note 4 from **J**
Bars 82, 83. Fingering in **J** accords with **S**. Fingering to bar 83 RH note 6 identical in **D**.
Bar 84. Fingering '2' identical in **J**
Bars 85–167. **A**: indicated as repeat of bars 17–84 then 1–15
Bars 121–136.
> **D**: RH contains following variant, notated in pencil in Dubois' hand:

Bar 134. Fingering from **D**
Bar 135. RH note 2: fingering identical in **D**

Bars 150–152.
   Bar 150 RH note 1: fingering identical in **J**. Bar 150 RH note 4, bar 151 RH note 2: fingering identical in **D**. Bar 151 RH note 6, bar 152: fingering from **D**.
Bars 169–172.
   D, **J**: LH fingering contrasts with that in **S** but together the sources yield the following:

Bars 173, 176.
   Fingering in **J** corresponds with that in **S**
Bar 174. LH notes 1, 4: fingering identical in **J**
Bar 175. LH note 5: fingering identical in **J**
Bars 175, 176, 177.
   RH slur by analogy with bar 174
Bar 177. LH note 1: fingering identical in **J**
Bar 181. RH fingering identical in **J**
Bars 181–183.
   LH slur by analogy with bars 177–179
Bar 183. **A**, **F**, **G**: no ♯ to f^2 RH chord 3; added in **E**, **S**
Bar 186. **F**, **G**, **E**: no augmentation dot to RH note 1
Bars 190–204.
   Indicated in **A** as repeat of bars 2–15

WALTZ OP. 34 NO. 3

Sources

F¹ French first edition, first impression published within *Album des Pianistes* […] *10ᵉ Année*, 1st December 1838. M. Schlesinger, Paris, plate no. M.S.2717.3.
F² Corrected reprint of **F¹**, December 1838.
F = F¹,²
G German first edition based on **F²**, December 1838. Breitkopf & Härtel, Leipzig, plate no. 6034.
E English first edition based on **F²**, December 1838. Wessel & Co., London, plate no. W & Cº Nº 2282.
D Dubois copy of **F²**. [F-Pn: Rés.F.980 (III, 5/3)]
J Jędrzejewicz copy of **F²**. [Pl-Wtfc: M/175]
S Stirling copy of **F²**. [F-Pn: Rés Vma 241 (IV, 34/III)]

The principal source for this edition is **F²**. The absence of handwritten sources makes it impossible to determine Fontana's role in preparing this edition.

Bars 17, 18, 20.
   Fingering from **S**, **J**
Bars 17, 18, 19, 20, 94, 96, 108 *et seq.*
   LH crotchet rest added to clarify counterpoint
Bar 19. Fingering to RH note 1 from **S**, **J**; fingering to RH notes 4, 5 from **J**
Bars 28, 139, 140.
   F, **G**: no slur to LH chords 2–3; here as in **E** and by analogy with similar bars
Bar 48. ❋ from **E** and by analogy with bar 32
Bar 49. **F**: no ♭ to e, e^1 LH chord 2; added in **G**, **E**, **D**, **J**
Bars 56, 72. **F**, **G**: no ♮ to RH note 5 (cf. **E**)
Bars 60, 76. Upper auxiliary to ❤ RH note 1: eb^2 more suited to harmonic context than $e\natural^2$
Bar 92. **F**, **G**: no staccato dot to RH beat 3; here by analogy with bar 108 (see also **E**)

Bars 93, 109. **F**, **G**: no slur to RH notes 1–2; here by analogy with similar bars (see also **E**)
Bars 93, 95, 109.
   Slur to LH beats 2–3 positioned below the chords in all sources
Bar 100. ❋ from **G** and by analogy with bar 84
Bar 105. ❋ from **G**, **E**, and by analogy with bar 97
Bar 109. Slur to RH notes 1–2 from **E** and by analogy with similar bars
Bar 111. No RH/LH slur in any source; here as in similar bars
Bar 128. ❋ from **G**, **E**, and by analogy with bar 127
Bars 147–148.
   LH slur over barline above LH staff in all sources; here below LH staff in order to show its relevance to bass line
Bar 148. LH chord 3: d–f^1 in all sources. The upper note is almost certainly an engraver's error left uncorrected by Fontana; here as in LH chords 1, 2 and by analogy with bar 152.
Bars 151–152.
   No LH slur over barline in any source; here as in bars 147–148

WALTZ OP. 42

Sources

[A] Hypothetical autograph. *Stichvorlage* for **F**.
FP Proofs of **F**, corrected by Chopin. *Stichvorlage* for **G**. [New York, USA, private collection]
[FP] Hypothetical proofs of **F**. *Stichvorlage* for **E**.
F French first edition, June 1840. Pacini, Paris, plate no. 3708.
G German first edition, June 1840. Breitkopf & Härtel, Leipzig, plate no. 6419.
E English first edition, June 1840. Wessel & Co., London, plate no. W & Cº Nº 3559.
D Dubois copy of **F**. [F-Pn: Rés. F. 980 (III)]
J Jędrzejewicz copy of **F**. [PL-Wtfc: M/176]

Suggested filiation

The autograph that served as the basis for **F** has not been preserved. **FP** was enclosed with the letter dated 18 June 1840 sent by Chopin to Breitkopf & Härtel, and was used in the preparation of **G**. Comparison of **G** with **E** establishes that a similar source was also supplied to Wessel. It is unclear why significant differences exist between the original editions, texts which should, given their common origins, be virtually identical. It is probable that Chopin corrected each source separately and from memory, and that a good deal of time elapsed between each set of corrections. Furthermore, he did not add pedalling indications to the proofsheets intended for Leipzig, thus resulting in their absence from **G**. Analysis confirms that Chopin's correction of the proofs for **F** itself was the least careful. That is not surprising, for it was done only by the composer, whereas **FP** and the corresponding source used to prepare **E** were revised again by professional proof-readers.

The principal source for this edition is **F**.

Bar 1. *Vivace* from **E**; *p* from **FP**, **G**; fingering from **D**
Bars 9–40 *et seq.*
   FP, **F**, **G**: RH crotchets have downward stems and the quavers upward stems in bars 9–16; these directions are inverted in bars 17–40. Here (as in **E**) only the latter notation is used, as the change in stem direction has no musical significance.

Bar 10. LH chords 3, 4: in **FP** the chord B♭–d♭–g is distinguishable through the crossing out; this original version was changed by Chopin in all three original editions. By contrast, at the reprise of the theme in bar 182, this detail has not been corrected, either to avoid exact repetition through oversight, or owing to lapse of memory.

Bars 16, 23, 30. **FP**, **F**: slur over barline breaks at RH note 6, i.e. at end of system; here one continuous slur as in bars 188, 195, 202

Bar 24. Upward stem to RH note 1 by analogy with bar 196

Bar 38. c^1 to LH chords 2, 3 from **E**

Bars 52, 53. Fingering from **D**

Bars 57–71. Pedalling from **E** although errors in **E** in bars 64–65 have been corrected

Bar 58. **F** RH chord 3: staccato dot instead of $d♭^2$; here as in **FP**, **G**, **E**, **D**

Bars 58–59, 62–63, 67, 70–71. RH notated as follows in all sources:

Here, to clarify the counterpoint, crotchet 'doubling' has been added to RH note 1. The original notation allows various interpretations; note for example the solutions proposed by two editors:

A. Michałowski [Warsaw/Cracow, Gebethner & Wolff, 1924]:

A. Casella [Paris, Société Française d'Editions des Grands Classiques Musicaux, 1916]:

Bar 59. RH accent as in bar 58

Bars 80, 112, 172. c^1 to LH chord 2 from **FP**, **G**, **E**

Bars 87–88, 119–120. Pedalling from **E**

Bars 90–91. **F**, **FP**, **G**, **E**: RH slur ends RH note 5 bar 90; here slur over barline as in bars 94–95 in **E**

Bar 91. **F**, **FP**, **E**: incorrect $d♭^1$ in RH chord 4 (cf. **G**)

Bars 92–95, 95–96. RH slur from **E**

Bar 95. *f* from **FP**, **G**

Bars 97–103. *cresc.* from **E**

Bars 102–103. **F**: RH slur over barline ends after bar 102 although continuation to bar 103 (on new system) clearly intended

Bar 103. **E**: g^1, not $e♭^1$, in RH chord 1

Bar 105. *p* from **FP**, **G**

Bars 116–117. **E**: no break in RH slur, which continues until bar 123

Bar 119. *p* from **E**

Bars 131–133, 135. All sources: LH note 1 notated as dotted minim with upward and downward stems; here crotchet 'doubling', notated with upward stem only, added to clarify counterpoint

Bar 136. **FP**, **G**, **E**: RH slur breaks RH chord 1

Bar 138. **FP**, **F**: no ♭ to a♯ RH chord 6

Bar 156. **FP**, **F**: no ♮ to d♭ LH chord 2 (cf. bar 148)

Bar 158. **FP**, **G**, **E**: RH grace note notated as semiquaver. Arpeggio sign from **FP**, **D**.

Bar 160. **FP**, **F**: no ♮ to $d♭^1$ LH chord 2, $d♭^2$ RH chord 5 (cf. **G**, **E**)

Bar 162. **FP**, **F**: ♮s wrongly placed before $d♭^2$ (not $e♭^2$) in RH chord 2, $d♭^1$ (not $e♭^1$) in LH chord 3 (cf. **G**, **E**)

Bars 162–164. **FP**, **G**, **E**: RH slurring as follows:

Bar 164. Variant from **FP**, **G**, **E** is without doubt more musically successful than the correction introduced by Chopin in **F**

Bar 174. LH chords 2, 3: c^1 from **FP**, **G**, **E** and by analogy with bars 50, 82

Bar 182. See comment to bar 10

Bar 196. **FP**, **F**, **G** RH note 1: c^2 undoubtedly an engraver's error corrected by Chopin on the proofs destined for **E**

Bars 207–209. *dim.* from **E**

Bar 210. *sostenuto* from **FP**, **G**, **E**

Bar 212. Line added after beat 3 in **D** possibly to lengthen final note of bar; equally it could be pause mark (⌒)

Bar 217. **FP**, **F**: no ♮ to RH notes 1, 4; no ♭ to RH note 6 (cf. **D**, **G**, **E**). Fingering from **J**.

Bar 218. **FP**, **G**, **F**: no ♭ to RH note 3 (cf. **D**, **E**)

Bar 219. **FP**, **F**: no ♭ to RH notes 1, 5 (cf. **D**, **G**, **E**)

Bar 221. **FP**, **F**: no ♭ to RH notes 5, 6 (cf. **G**). Fingering from **E**.

Bars 223, 224, 225, 226. Accent from **FP**, **G**

Bar 227. LH slur from **E**, **G**; accent by analogy with similar bars in **G**

Bars 229–231. **F**, **E**: RH slur ends bar 230 RH chord 5 (cf. **FP**, **G**)

Bar 230. ======= from **FP**

Bar 231. **FP**, **F**, **G**: $a♭$ not $b♭$ in LH chord 2 (cf. **E**)

Bars 232–235. **F**: RH slur over barlines begins bar 233 RH chord 1 (cf. **FP**, **E**)

Bar 236. LH chord 3: notated in **FP**, **F** as crotchet followed by quaver rest; in **E** as crotchet, with no quaver rest to follow; in **G** as quaver followed by quaver rest (as here). **FP**, **F**, **G**: no 𝄐 after beat 3.

Bar 239. *leggiero* from **FP**, **G**, **E** (**F** has only *p*, also present in **E**)

Bars 243–244. **D** contains virtually illegible line drawn in Chopin's hand, then the word *octava*, indicating extension of line to higher octave

Bar 244. Wedge staccato from **FP**

Bars 244–261. No pedalling in **FP**, **G**, **E**

Bars 250–251. **FP**, **F**: RH slur over barline ends after bar 250 although continuation to bar 251 (on new system) clearly intended; here as in **G**

Bars 254–255, 255–256. RH slurs over barline by analogy with bars 251–252

Bar 256. **F**: erroneous ♭ to f^2 RH chord 2, corrected to ♮ in **J**, whereas **E** has $g♭^2$, not f^2 (cf. **FP**, **G**)

Bars 259–261.
Alternative slurring in **FP**, **G**: RH slur breaks at bar 259 RH chord 1; then follow two single slurs from bars 259/260 RH chord 2 to bars 260/261 RH chord 1

Bar 260. **FP**, **G**: no ab^2 RH chords 2, 3. **F**, **E**: no ♮ to db^1 LH chord 2.

Bar 261. RH note 1: staccato dot from **FP**. All sources: LH chord 2 db^1–eb^1–g^1; redundant g^1 removed here as it is also played by RH (cf. variants in bars 49, 81, 173, 269).

Bar 268. **F**: ♭♮, not cb^1, in LH chord 3; this was corrected by Chopin in **FP** (cf. also **G**, **E**)

Bars 269–285.
Dynamic progression differs in all sources. In **FP** and **G**, the dynamics generally grow louder: *f* in bar 269 leads to *ff* at bar 273, reinforcing LH octave doubling; this is followed by *crescendo* from bar 277, culminating in second *ff* at bar 285. In **E**, *f* appears at bar 277; *crescendo* beginning there lasts only until following bar; *ff* is not used until bar 285, where it culminates in octave doubling of LH part.

Bars 277, 278, 279, 280.
F: no accent; positioning of accent in **FP** ambiguous; **G** has long accent below RH notes 5–6; here as in **E**

Bar 281. **FP**, **F**, **G**: no c^2 in RH chord 4 (cf. **E**)

Bars 283, 284.
Bar 283 RH note 4, bar 284 RH notes 2, 6 have additional, handwritten stems in **D** indicating articulation by LH; here shown by '*m.s.*'

Bars 284–285.
Original version visible through corrections in **FP**, featuring ab to RH note 6 bar 284 and Ab to LH note 1 bar 285; cf. **E** (see variant in bar 284)

Bars 286, 287.
Accent from **E**

WALTZ OP. 64 NO. 1

Sources

A¹	Autograph sketch. [F-Pn: Ms. 111 A]
A²	Autograph incipit. [E-VALm]
A³	Autograph. [D-BNu: UB 281/2]
A⁴	Autograph. [F-Pn: Ms. 111 B]
A⁵	Autograph presented to Juliette de Caraman, July 1847. [GB-Lcm: Ms. 4224]
A⁶	Autograph. *Stichvorlage* for **F¹**. [Basel, Switzerland, private collection]
[FP]	Hypothetical proofs of **F¹**. *Stichvorlage* for **G¹**, **G²**.
F¹	French first edition, November 1847. Brandus & Co., Paris, plate no. B et Cie 4743.(1).
F²	Reprint of **F¹**, without plate no., in *Album de piano de la Gazette musicale 1848*.
F = F¹,²	
G¹	German first edition published within volume containing entire opus, November 1847. Breitkopf & Härtel, plate no. 7721.
G²	Separately published German first edition, August 1849. Breitkopf & Härtel, Leipzig, plate no. 7715.
G = G¹,²	
E¹	English first edition, April 1848. Cramer, Beale & Co., London, plate no. 4368.
E²	English second edition, September 1848. Wessel & Co., London, plate no. W & C⁰ N° 6321.
E = E¹,²	
D	Dubois copy of **F¹**. [F-Pn: Rés. F. 980 (III)]
S	Stirling copy of **F¹**. [F-Pn: Vma 241 (V)]

Suggested filiation

There are numerous differences between the autograph sources, but also many commonalities between **A³⁻⁵**. **A⁶** was the basis of **F¹**, which was twice corrected by Chopin. **G¹** was based on the French proofs, which Clara Schumann corrected during the preparation of **G¹** and possibly also **G²** (see her letter of 9 September 1847 to Hermann Härtel, in Monica Stegemann, '…daß Gott mir ein Talent geschenkt': Clara Schumanns Briefe an Hermann Härtel und Richard und Helene Schöne (Zürich und Mainz: Atlantis Musikbuch-Verlag, 1997, p. 52)). **E¹** and **E²** were based on the definitive version of **F¹**.

The principal source for this edition is **F¹**, which was the last source to be corrected by the composer. A second version, based on **A³** but also including readings from **A⁴** and **A⁵**, is reproduced in the Appendix.

Version based on **F¹**

D contains a number of indications in two different hands, neither of them Chopin's. Only one fingering typical of Chopin has been reproduced here.

Bar 1. The variant – almost certainly Chopin's own – was notated by Dubois not as transcribed here but as follows: '*tr*' underneath first note, '4 mesures' above it. **E¹**: *pp* at end of bar.

Bar 12. **G²**: no ⁓ to RH note 2

Bars 24, 25. Fingering from **D**

Bar 20. **G**: no ⁓ to RH note 3. **A⁶**: trill to RH note 3

Bars 25, 97, 113.
E²: 𝄂. to beat 1, ✱ to beat 3

Bar 32. ⎯⎯⎯ incorrectly begins RH note 3 in **F**, **G¹**, **E²**, bar 32 RH note 1 in **E¹**, bar 33 note 2 in **G²**; here as in **A⁶**

Bar 35–36b. Slur over barline by analogy with bars 35–36a

Bar 36b. **A⁶**, **F**, **E¹** have double barline after beat 2, and, underneath, 'fine'. These are the legacy of the original *da capo* form discernible in **A¹,³⁻⁵**. Having modified the form while writing out **A⁶**, Chopin forgot to remove these redundant markings. Pedalling as in bar 36a.

Bars 36b–37. **G¹**: Tie to RH ab^1's over barline

Bars 45–53. **G¹**: RH slur begins bar 45 note 3, ends bar 53 note 1

Bar 50. **A³⁻⁶**, **G** LH note 1: *c*, not *C*

Bar 51. **G** RH note 2: g^2, not gb^2

Bar 53. *p* from **A⁶**

Bars 54, 55. Fingering from **S**

Bars 61–68. RH slurring differs in the sources: **A⁶** contains RH slurs to bars 61–63, 64–68, while the editions lack a RH slur in bars 61–63. Here by analogy with bars 37–43.

Bar 77. *fz* from **A⁶**

Bar 91. ⎯⎯⎯ from **A⁶**

Bar 92. **F**, **G**, **E**: *tr* to RH note 3; ⁓ here as in bar 20. **G** has LH version originates from **A⁶**, **[FP]**:

Bar 93. **S** has RH variant marked in ink:

Bar 104.   ⸺   incorrectly begins RH note 3 in all printed sources; here as in **A⁶**
Bars 117–118.   ⸺   from **A⁶**
Bars 120, 121. Fingering from **S**
Bar 123. Liaison from **D**
Bar 124. **A⁶**: no ❊

WALTZ OP. 64 NO. 2

Sources

A¹	Autograph sketch. [F-Po: Rés. 50 (1)]
A²	Autograph. Formerly in possession of Rothschild family. [F-Pn: Ms. 114]
A³	Autograph. *Stichvorlage* for **F**. [Basel, Switzerland, private collection]
[FP]	Hypothetical proofs of **F**. *Stichvorlage* for **G¹**, **G²**.
F	French first edition, November 1847. Brandus & Co., Paris, plate no. B & Cⁱᵉ 4743.(2).
G¹	German first edition published within volume containing entire opus, November 1847. Breitkopf & Härtel, plate no. 7721.
G²	Separately published German first edition, August 1849. Breitkopf & Härtel, Leipzig, plate no. 7716.
G = G¹,²	
E¹	English first edition, April 1848. Cramer, Beale & Co., London, plate no. 4369.
E²	English second edition, September 1848. Wessel & Co., London, plate no. W & Cº Nº 6322.
E = E¹,²	
D	Dubois copy of **F**. [F-Pn: Rés. F. 980 (III)]
S	Stirling copy of **F**. [F-Pn: Vma 241 (V)]

Suggested filiation

The filiation of Op. 64 No. 2 is generally identical to that of No. 1, although Clara Schumann's corrections are of greater significance here. **D** contains some slurs notated in an unidentified hand, which for the most part seem to have been copied from **G¹,²** as well as from other post-1849 German sources. Consequently they do not feature as variants in the principal text, but appear only in the Critical Commentary.

The principal source for this edition is **F**, which was the last source to be corrected by Chopin. A second version, based on the little-known **A²**, is provided in the Appendix.

Version based on F

Bars 5–6.   ⸺   from **A³**
Bars 7, 8, 136. **F**, **E¹**: slur linking RH grace note and RH chord 3 can be attributed to the French engraver; here no slur as in **A³**
Bars 8, 9. RH slurring from **A³**; single RH slur spans both bars in all printed sources
Bars 9, 137.   ⸺   from **A³**
Bars 10–11. RH slur from **A³**
Bars 12–18. All printed sources: RH slur over barlines begins erroneously bar 13 RH note 1; here as in **A³**
Bars 12, 18 *et seq*. LH crotchet rest added to clarify counterpoint
Bar 22. No pedalling in **F**, **G**, **E¹**; here as in **A³**, **E²**

Bars 25, 153.   ⸺   by analogy with **A³** bar 8
Bars 27–28, 29–30. **D**: handwritten tie over barline respectively to $c\sharp^2$s (bar 27 RH note 2, bar 28 RH note 1) and b^1s (bar 29 RH note 2, bar 30 RH note 1)
Bars 29–31. Pedalling from **A³**. **F**, **G²**, **E¹**: ❊ positioned after final LH note in bars 29, 31, which is harmonically incorrect. Bar 30: no pedalling in any printed source.
Bars 31–32.   ⸺   from **A³**
Bar 32. **A¹⁻³**, **G** LH note 1: $c\sharp$, not $C\sharp$
Bar 33. No change of tempo in any source, although in **A³**, **F**, **E** the parallel bar (bar 161) features such a change; thus it is likely that the omission in bar 33 resulted from an oversight on Chopin's part
Bars 39, 103, 167. **F**: RH slur incorrectly begins RH note 2; here as in **A³**, **E**
Bar 40. Fingering from **D**
Bars 40, 56 *et seq*. **A³**, **F**, **E¹**: no $\sharp$ to RH note 6 (see also **A²** version in Appendix)
Bars 45, 61, 109, 125, 173. **A¹⁻³**, **G**: no a^1 LH chord 2
Bar 49. No pedalling in **F**, **G**, **E**; here as in **A³**
Bar 64. **A³**, **G**: new key signature has 4 rather than 5 ♭s
Bars 66–67. **D**: tie over barline to RH eb^2s
Bars 68–69, 72–73, 84–85.   ⸺   from **A³**
Bars 68–69, 72–73, 88–89. Tie and LH slur beneath staff from **A³**; Chopin appears to have overlooked the engraving errors and omissions in **F** here when correcting the proofs
Bars 70–71. **G**: tie over barline to RH f^2s, also marked in pencil in **D**
Bars 70–72.   ⸺   from **A³**
Bars 71–72. Tie over barline to LH gb^1s from **S**
Bar 73. **A³**, **F**, **G²**, **E**: no augmentation dot to f LH chord 1; here as in **G¹** and by analogy with bars 68, 72
Bars 75–76. **G**: RH db^3s tied. **A³**: no ❊; ❊ positioned at end of bar 75 in **F**, **G**, **E**. Chopin, when correcting the proofs of **F**, forgot to re-position the ❊ after changing bar 76 LH note 1 (see comment below).
Bar 76. **A³**, **G** LH beat 1: gb, not chord bb–eb^1–bb^1. **G²**: erroneous tie to RH notes 1, 2.
Bars 76–77. **G¹**: tie to RH db^3s over barline, also marked in pencil in **D**
Bars 77, 78. Fingering from **S**
Bars 81–82. **F**, **E**: no tie over barline to RH f^2s; here as in **A³**
Bar 85. **A³**: 𝄢. positioned beneath beat 1. It is advisable to use pedalling marked in **F**, i.e. holding eb LH beat 1 to end of beat 2.
Bar 88. Pedalling by analogy with bar 72. **A³**, **F**, **G²**, **E**: no augmentation dot to c^1 LH chord 1; here as in bar 72.
Bar 89. No pedalling in any printed source; here ❊ from **A³** (cf. 𝄢 under LH note 1)
Bars 91–92, 92–93. **G**: tie over barline to RH db^3s; **D** also contains second tie marked in pencil
Bars 92, 93. LH slur from **S**
Bar 93. **F**, **E¹** LH chord 1: no ♮ to gb^1
Bar 96. **F**, **E¹**: no ♮ to RH note 6
Bar 97.   ⸺   as in bar 33
Bars 103–104. No ⸺ in any printed source; here as in bars 39–40

Bar 106.   **F**, **G**, **E¹**: no pedalling; here as in **A³**, **E²**

Bar 131.   **F**, **G¹**, **E**: no ✱; here as in **A³**, **G²**

Bar 136.   **F**, **G**, **E²**: no RH slur; here as in **A³**, **E¹**

Bars 154, 155, 156, 157, 158.
       Fingering from **S**

Bars 157–158.
       No LH slur over barline in any source; here by analogy with bars 29–30. **D**: tie over barline to RH b^1s.

Bars 157, 159.
       F: ✱ erroneously placed after beat 3; here as in **A³**

Bars 159–160.
       A³, **G**: no $g\sharp^1$ bar 159 RH chord 5, bar 160 RH chord 1.

Bar 160.   **A³**, **G**: $c\sharp$, not $C\sharp$, LH note 1

Bar 168.   **F**, **G**, **E¹**: no pedalling; here as in **A³**

Bar 188.   No pedalling in any printed source; here as in **A³**

Bar 189.   **A³**, **F**, **G**, **E¹**: no a^1 to LH chord beat 3; here as in **E²** and by analogy with similar bars

WALTZ OP. 64 NO. 3

Sources

A¹   Autograph sketch. [F-Po: Rés. 50 (1)]

A²   Autograph. *Stichvorlage* for **F**. [Basel, Switzerland, private collection]

[FP]   Hypothetical proofs of **F**. *Stichvorlage* for **G¹**, **G²**.

F   French first edition, November 1847. Brandus & Co., Paris, plate no. B & Cⁱᵉ 4743.(3).

G¹   German first edition published within volume containing entire opus, November 1847. Breitkopf & Härtel, plate no. 7721.

G²   Separately published German first edition, August 1849. Breitkopf & Härtel, Leipzig, plate no. 7717.

G = G¹,²

E¹   English first edition, September 1848. Wessel & Co., London, plate no. W & Cº Nº 6323.

E²   English second edition, 1848/1849. Cramer, Beale & Co., London, plate no. 4502.

E = E¹,²

D   Dubois copy of **F**. [F-Pn: Rés. F. 980 (III)]

Suggested filiation

The filiation is identical to that of Op. 64 No. 2, apart from the existence of only two autographs.

The principal source for this edition is **F**, the last source to be corrected by Chopin.

Bar 9.   Pedalling from **A²**

Bars 13–14.   LH slur from **A²**, **E²**

Bars 13–14 *et seq*.
       F, **G**, **E**: ✱ at end of bar 13 and ℘ₑ𝒹. at beginning of bar 14, resulting from earlier version of LH which was also changed by Chopin in **A²** after first French proofs had been engraved; in correcting the plates, the French engraver overlooked these pedalling changes. Here as in **A²**.

Bar 15.   **F**, **E**: RH slur over barline ends RH note 4, thus next slur starts RH note 5; here as in **A²**. Fingering from **A¹**.

Bar 16.   ⟨ from **A²**

Bars 31, 124.   **F**, **G**, **E**: RH slur over barline ends RH note 4, thus next slur starts RH note 5

Bar 42.   ♭ to RH note 2 present only in **A¹**

Bar 49.   RH notes 3, 4: g^1, g^1 in **A¹,²** and (presumably) **[FP]**; g^1, $a\flat^1$ in **G**

Bars 57–60.   In **A²** (presumably also **[FP]**) the only $d\flat^2$ preceded by ♮ sign is bar 57 RH note 2. In **G**, ♮s appear to all $d\flat^2$s here, including those in trill bars 59–60. Chopin changed ♮ to ♭ in bar 57 when correcting second set of French proofs.

Bars 57–62.   Broken *crescendo* line from **A²**

Bar 60.   **G**: LH chord 3 identical to LH chord 1 (almost certainly Clara Schumann's correction)

Bars 61–64.   LH slur over barlines ends after bar 62 LH chord 3 in **F**, **E²**, while **G** lacks slur; here as in **A²**, **E¹**

Bar 66.   Pedalling from **A²**; in all printed sources, ✱ is positioned at end of bar

Bar 72.   Pedalling from **A²**.

Bars 73–77.   **F**, **G**, **E²**: two LH slurs over barlines, from bar 73 LH note 2 to bar 75 LH note 3, then from bar 76 LH note 1 to bar 77 LH note 1; here one continuous slur as in **A²**, **E¹**

Bars 75–76.   **F**, **E²**: no RH tie over barline to g^1s; here as in **A²**, **G**, **E¹**

Bar 77.   All printed sources: LH slur ends LH note 1, then new slur starts LH note 2; here as in **A²**

Bars 80–83.   Erroneous RH slurring in all printed sources. **F**, **G²**, **E**: RH slur ends bar 81 RH chord 3, thus new RH slur starts bar 82 RH chord 1. **G¹**: single RH slur over barlines. Here as in **A²**.

Bars 80–84.   **A²**, **F**, **G**, **E**: LH slur over barlines ends bar 83 LH note 6; here as in bar 91–92

Bar 83.   Crotchet rest added to clarify rhythm

Bar 92.   **F**, **G**, **E**: tie to c^1s RH chords 1, 2 (engraving error); here as in **A²**

Bar 98.   **F**: no ♭ to d^2 RH chord 3. ⟩ by analogy with bar 106.

Bar 109.   **A²**, **G**: no *sostenuto*

Bar 121.   **F**, **E¹**: no ♮ to $d\flat^3$ RH note 4

Bar 122.   **F**, **E¹**: no ♮ to $d\flat^2$ RH note 3

Bar 140.   ⟨ from **A²**. Fingering from **D**.

Bar 142.   Arpeggio sign from **A²**. **F**, **G²**, **E**: pedalling is incorrect, with only one pedal indication for whole of bar; here as in **A²** (**G¹**: no pedalling).

Bar 143.   **A²**, **G**: no ♮ to RH note 6 (**G¹**: erroneous ♮ to RH note 5)

Bars 143, 144, 146, 147.
       F, **G**, **E**: ✱ positioned after LH beat 3; here as in **A²**

Bars 144–145.   ⟨ across barline from **A³**; in **F**, **G**, **E** hairpin to bar 145 RH notes 1–2 only

Bar 151.   Fingering from **A¹**

Bars 153–156.   ⟨ from **A²**

Bars 160–164.
       A², **G**: LH chord 3 identical to LH chord 2 in bars 160, 162, 164; LH chord 2 identical to LH chord 3 in bars 161, 163. Chopin refined text while correcting second set of proofs for Brandus edition.

Bar 161.   Long accent from **A²**

Bar 171.   **F**, **G**, **E**: >, not long accent; here as in **A²**

WALTZ in B minor (composed 1829)

Sources

C¹	Copy, attributed to Wojciech Żywny. [Pl-Kj]
C²	Copy, prepared by unidentified copyist. [F-Pn: D 10812]
P	Polish first edition, 1842. I. Wildt, Cracow, plate no. 3, prepared from autograph notated in 1844 in album of Countess Plater.
E¹	English first edition, July 1853. Wessel & Co., London, plate no. W & Cº Nº 8015.
E²	English second edition. April 1854. J. J. Ewer, London, without plate no.
F	French first edition, July 1855. J. Meissonnier Fils, Paris, plate no. J. M. 3526 (version by J. Fontana).
G	German first edition, July 1855. A. M. Schlesinger, Berlin, plate no. S. 4395 (version by J. Fontana).

Suggested filiation

According to Oskar Kolberg (1881), **C¹** dates from 1829. **C²** was based on a later manuscript, but one that pre-dates the 1844 source used to prepare **P**. **E**^{1,2} reproduces the text of **P**. **G** and **F** seem to amalgamate the text of the first three cited sources.

There are significant differences between the two copies and the editions. Three versions are given here, based on **C¹**, **C²** and **P** respectively.

Version based on C¹

Bars 4, 10, 42.	Accent to RH note 2 from **C²** and by analogy with bar 2
Bars 7, 39.	Accent to RH note 3 from **C²** and by analogy with bar 6
Bar 9.	RH slur from **C²**
Bars 11, 43.	RH slur by analogy with bar 3
Bars 15, 46.	**C¹**: LH note 1 notated as minim with upward and downward stems; here, to clarify counterpoint, minim doubled by crotchet and augmentation dot added
Bar 36.	*fz* to RH note 2 by analogy with bar 34
Bars 36–38.	RH slurring by analogy with bars 5–6 and 34–35
Bars 38–48.	Notated in **C¹** as repeat of bars 6–16b
Bar 41.	RH slur as in bar 9
Bar 60.	**C¹** RH note 2: e^2 (obvious error; cf. **C²**, **P**)
Bars 61–64.	RH slurs by analogy with bars 53–56
Bar 77.	**C¹** LH chord 2: no ♮ to $d\sharp^1$ (obvious omission; cf. **C²**, **P**)

Version based on C²

Bars 2, 39.	**C²**: erroneous reverse accent to RH note 2; here > by analogy with similar bars
Bar 16a.	**C²**: ⌒ to RH note 1; *fine* marked at end of bar. This ⌒ serves to indicate final note of Waltz during *da capo* repeat; as present edition prints *da capo* in full, ⌒ and *fine* are omitted.
Bar 27.	**C²**: LH chord 2 $f\sharp$–a–g^1, LH chord 3 a–g^1; here as in bar 19
Bar 34.	**C²** LH note 1: e (obvious error; cf. **C¹**, **P**)
Bar 38.	**C²**: accent to RH beat 1; here as in bar 6
Bar 43.	RH slur as in bars 3, 11
Bar 44.	**C²**: illegible ornament, possibly ⁓; ∞ better suits melodic context
Bars 44–45.	RH slur over barline as in bars 12–13
Bars 46.	**C²**: RH note 3 $b\sharp^1$, not b^1; RH note 4 $c\sharp^2$, not c^2 (certainly incorrect); here as in bar 14. LH note 1 (grace note): F♯, not E (also erroneous).
Bar 49.	Slur from **P** and by analogy with bar 51
Bar 55.	Slur to RH notes 2–3 as in bar 61
Bar 56.	**C²**: RH note 3 $d\sharp^2$, not $c\sharp^2$ (possibly erroneous); here $c\sharp^2$ as in **C¹**, **P**
Bar 60.	$c\sharp^1$ to LH chords beats 2, 3 from **C¹**, **P** and as in bar 58
Bar 62.	**C²**: incorrect top note $a\sharp^1$ in LH chords 2, 3 (cf. **C¹**, **P**)
Bars 63, 64.	Slur to RH notes 2–3 by analogy with similar bars
Bar 67.	**C²**: slur ends RH chord 6; here slur over barline as in bars 65–66, 73–74
Bar 68.	**C²**: incorrect $f\sharp^1$ in RH chord 1; here $a\sharp^1$ as in **P** and by analogy with bar 66
Bar 70.	**C²**: no $c\sharp^1$ in LH chords 2, 3; here as in **P**
Bars 70, 71.	Staccato dot to RH note 1 by analogy with bar 72
Bar 74.	Accent to RH note 3 as in bars 66, 68, 76
Bars 75–77.	**C²**: no slur in bar 75, then slur from beat 1 bar 76 to beat 3 bar 77 ; here slur over barline for bars 75–76 (by analogy to bars 65–66, 73–74) and slur for bar 77 (as in bar 78)
Bar 76.	**C²**: RH chord 2 notated incorrectly as crotchet
Bar 80.	**C²** LH chord 1: $a\sharp^1$–$c\sharp^1$–$a\sharp^1$ top note – also held by RH – possibly erroneous
Bars 81–86.	Indicated in **C²** as reprise of bars 1–16a (see comment to bar 16a)

Version based on P

Bars 6–7.	**P**: no tie over barline to RH d^3s; here as in **C**^{1,2}
Bar 7.	**P**: $c\sharp^1$ in LH chords 2, 3; here as in **C**^{1,2}
Bar 16b.	**P**: no 'Fine' specified, end of *da capo* ambiguous; here as in **C¹**
Bar 17.	**P**: no double barline or right-facing repeat sign
Bars 22, 27.	Long accent by analogy with bars 23, 26
Bar 29.	Erroneous $c\sharp^1$, not e^1, in LH chords 2, 3; here as in bar 17
Bar 34.	Erroneous ♯, not ♮, to RH note 2; here as in **C**^{1,2}
Bar 36.	**P** LH note 1: d, not B (probably an engraving error); here as in **C**^{1,2}, **F**, **G**. Accent to RH note 2 by analogy with bar 34.
Bars 57, 58.	RH slurs by analogy with bars 65, 66
Bar 62.	**P** RH chord 1: no $c\sharp^1$; here by analogy with bar 64
Bar 67.	RH slur as in bar 65
Bar 72.	**P**: RH chord 4 $f\sharp^1$–$f\sharp^2$, LH chord 3 $f\sharp$–$a\sharp$–e^1 (almost certainly erroneous); here as in **C²** and by analogy with bar 55
Bar 74.	RH slur as in bar 76
Bars 74, 76.	**P** RH chord 1: no ♮ to $g\sharp^2$ (obvious omission; cf. **C**^{1,2})

WALTZ in D♭ major (composed 1829)

Sources

F	French first edition, July 1855. J. Meissonnier Fils, Paris, plate no. J. M. 3527 (version by J. Fontana).
G	German first edition, July 1855. A. M. Schlesinger, Berlin, plate no. S. 4396 (version by J. Fontana).

As no manuscript source is extant, this edition is based on **F**.

Bars 1, 5, 9, 13.	**F**, **G**: no ♭ to $g\flat^2$ RH note 6
Bar 5.	RH slur as in bar 1
Bar 16.	Crotchet stem to RH note 1, RH crotchet rests, RH slur as in bar 8

Bar 29. ======= as in bar 21
Bar 31. *dim.* as in bar 23
Bars 34, 35, 58, 59.
RH slur as in bars 42, 43. **F** has >s to RH note 1 in bars 34, 58, 59 (as also in **G**) and long accent to RH note 1 bar 35 (cf. **G**'s >); long accents here seem more appropriate in context.
Bars 37, 61. **F**, **G**: slur to LH notes 2–3, not LH notes 1–4; here as in bars 45, 69
Bars 38, 39, 62, 63.
No LH slur in **F**, **G**; here as in bars 45, 46
Bar 49. Slur to RH notes 2–4 as in bar 53
Bars 50, 54. **F**, **G** RH chords 3, 4: tied ab^1's given as ♩ (**F**: augmentation dot to crotchet erroneously omitted in bar 50)
Bar 72. **F**, **G** contain crotchet rest to beat 3 and indication '*Fine o da capo il Valzo*'. Finishing piece at end of trio was almost certainly Fontana's idea, but returning to the beginning is consistent with the ABA form typical of Chopin's other waltzes.

WALTZ in E major (composed 1829/30)

Sources

P¹ Polish first edition, 1861. Published in *Album Towarzystwa Muzycznego we Lwowie*, Lvov, plate no. 343.
P² Polish second edition, 1871. W. Chaberski, Cracow, without plate no.

Suggested filiation

P¹ was based on an 1829 autograph, now lost. The text of **P²** was probably based on **P¹**, but with minor corrections to the phrasing, articulation and dynamics. However, **P²** does not distinguish the trio as such and lacks the first phrase of the introduction (bars 1–4) in the *da capo* (which is otherwise printed in full) — an omission which is detrimental to the musical structure.

The principal source for this edition is **P¹**.

Bars 0–1, 2–5.
LH slurs by analogy with bars 1–2
Bars 19, 51. RH slur as in bar 11
Bars 27–28. LH slur across barline as in bars 35–36
Bar 61. Staccato dot to RH note 4 by analogy with bars 62, 63, 64
Bar 64. > to RH note 1 and staccato dot to LH note 1 as in bars 62, 63
Bar 66. RH slur as in bar 58

WALTZ in A♭ major (composed 1830)

Sources

A Autograph. Album of Mrs Le Brun. [Pl-Wtm: 12/Ch]
G German first edition, 1902. Based on autograph (now lost) notated in album of Emilia Elsner. Breitkopf & Härtel, Leipzig, Klav. Bibl. 23183 II.

As the two sources differ considerably, two versions are given here.

Version based on A

Bars 7, 31. **A**: no ♭ to RH note 6

Bars 16a, 13b–16b, 24b, 37–40, 47–48a/b.
RH slurring in accordance with musical context
Bar 18. **A**: no c^1 to LH chord 2; here as in **G**
Bars 20–24a. **A**: RH slur over barline seems to end after bar 23 RH note 6, although extension to bar 24a note 1 probably intended (as here)
Bars 25–40. Not given in **A**, as *Dal segno al fine e poi* marked after bar 24b denotes reprise of bars 1–16

Version based on G

Bar 5. **G**: LH chords beats 2 and 3 contain *g*, not *e♭* (certainly an error); here as in bars 21, 53. Version of chord in **A** (with *g*, not *b♭*) is more convincing.
Bars 11, 12. **G**: no ♭ to RH note 5
Bars 31–32, 63–64.
G: no RH *ottava* indication
Bar 48. **G** RH note 6: redundant ♭ instead of ♮ (cf. **A**)

WALTZ in E minor (composed 1830)

Sources

P¹ Polish first edition, 1868. Joseph Kaufmann, Warsaw, plate no. J 159 K.
P² Corrected reprint of **P¹**.
P³ Corrected reprint of **P²**.
P = **P¹⁻³**
G German first edition, 1868. Les Fils de B. Schott, Mainz, plate no. 19551.

Suggested filiation

The copy of **P¹** in the Schott Archives, containing both handwritten reviser's corrections and engraver's annotations, served as the *Stichvorlage* for **G**. It is likely that certain elements in **P²** derived from the source used in preparing **P¹**. **P³** contains further minor improvements with regard to **P²**.

The principal source for this edition is **P²**.

Bars 4–7. Pedalling could alternatively be used at beginning of each bar
Bars 4–8. All sources: separate RH slur for bar 4 (located at end of system in **P**), then RH slur from bar 5 to bar 8. Given that the separate slur for bar 4 makes no musical sense, here the RH slur extends from bar 4 to 8; alternatively, a single slur to bars 1–8 would be musically justifiable.
Bar 9. Staccato dots to RH notes 1–4 from **G**
Bars 13, 14. Staccato dot to RH note 2 by analogy with bar 15
Bar 18. All sources: RH slur ends RH note 5, no staccato dot to note 5; here as in bar 10
Bars 36, 37. Staccato dot to LH note 1 from **G**, **P³**
Bars 43, 51, 115, 123.
No RH slur in any source; here as in bars 11, 19
Bar 50. Staccato dot to RH note 5 by analogy with bars 10, 42, 138
Bar 60. **P¹,²**: 𝄢 omitted after LH beat 3; here 𝄢 as in **P³**, **G**
Bars 63–64. All sources: erroneous single pedal indication; pedal change here as in bars 79–80
Bar 67. LH note 1: octave e–e^1 in all sources (attributable to Polish engraver's error in reading manuscript); here as in bars 59, 83

Bar 80.	All sources: RH slur ends RH note 2; here as in bars 63–64
Bars 89–112.	All sources repeat these bars in full because of the following differences: fingering '4' to LH note 6 bar 89; d♯¹–g♯¹ RH chord 1 bar 90 (**P²** only); ⸢, not ⸢⸝, bar 92 LH note 1; LH slur extended over barline to bar 96 note 1; no ⸺ bar 99; ✲ under LH note 6 bar 105; ℘. under LH note 1 bar 106; no RH slur in bars 109–110; RH slur from bar 111 RH note 4 to bar 112 RH chord 1. Given Chopin's normal notational practice, it is unlikely that these bars were repeated in his manuscript. These 'variants' probably stem from the engraver and are not included here as they have no musical significance.
Bar 92.	**P²** RH chord 1: d♯¹–g♯¹ (incoherent correction of **P¹** version; see also comment above); here as in bar 90 (cf. also **P³**)
Bar 97.	It is advisable to arpeggiate RH chord (cf. bar 57)
Bar 105.	No ℘. marking in any source; here pedalling as in bar 107–108 (see also comment to bars 89–112)
Bar 111.	**P¹,²** LH note 2: d♯ (obvious error); here f♯ as in **P³** and **G**
Bar 115.	**P**: no ✲; here as in similar bars
Bars 115–116.	All sources: erroneous 𝄢 after LH beat 3 bar 115 and redundant 𝄞 after LH beat 1 bar 116
Bars 116–118.	No pedalling in any source; here as in bars 12–14, 44–46
Bar 120.	All sources: separate beaming for two last RH quavers results from prolongation of *ottava* line from bar 115 to bar 120 note 4; here as in bars 16, 48
Bar 122.	**P**: no slur to LH beat 2, 3, no staccato dot to RH note 5; here as in **G** and by analogy with bars 10, 42, 114
Bar 124.	♮ to LH chord 1 from **P¹**, **G** (wrongly removed in **P²,³**)
Bar 125.	**P¹,²**: no ♮ to RH note 3 (♮ erroneously situated after note 3 in **P³**)
Bars 126, 127.	Accent to RH note 1 by analogy with bar 125
Bar 128.	Accent to LH chord 2 by analogy with bars 125, 126, 127

WALTZ in G♭ major (composed 1832)

Sources

A¹	Autograph, dated 'Paris 8/8 32'. [Formerly in US-NH. Sold at Christie's, 1992, unknown owner]
A²	Autograph, 1833. [Château de Thoiry, Yvelines, France, private collection]
C	Copy, prepared by unidentified copyist, based on **A¹**. [F-Pn: D 10812]
F	French first edition, July 1855. J. Meissonnier Fils, Paris, plate no. J.M. 3527 (version by J. Fontana).
G	German first edition, July 1855. A. M. Schlesinger, Berlin, plate no. S. 4396) (version by J. Fontana).

As the autographs differ considerably, two versions are given here.

Version based on A¹

Bar 5.	**A¹**: no ♭ to RH note 7
Bars 7–8a.	RH slur over barline from **A²**
Bars 7–8b.	RH slur over barline by analogy with bars 7–8a
Bar 8a.	**A¹**: RH note 1 notated octave higher as *ottava* sign ends before bar 8
Bars 8a/b.	No first-/second-time bars in **A¹**: Chopin gives only bar 8b, placing RH/LH right-facing repeat sign after LH chord 2
Bars 8b–9.	**A¹**: RH slur over barline incomplete, ending bar 9 RH note 2; here as in **C**
Bars 9–11.	**A¹**: RH slur over barlines incomplete, beginning bar 9 RH note 6 but then becoming confused with *ottava* line; here as in **C**
Bar 11.	**A¹**: no ♮ to RH note 6. Slur to RH notes 4–5 by analogy with bar 12.
Bar 15.	Slur to RH notes 6–7 from **C**
Bars 15–16a.	Slur over barline from **A²**
Bars 15–16b.	Slur over barline by analogy with bars 15–16a
Bar 16b.	**A¹**: minuscule line above RH note 5 could be staccato dot or possibly end of slur
Bars 23–24a/b.	RH slur over barline as in bars 39–40
Bar 30.	**F**, **G** RH chord 2: ♮ to c♭²
Bar 37.	Long accent to RH chord 1 as in bars 17, 19

Version based on A²

Bar 1.	RH slur as in bar 9
Bars 15–16.	RH slur over barline as in bars 7–8
Bars 23–24b.	RH slur over barline as in bars 23–24a
Bar 24b.	Accent to RH notes 4–5 from **A¹**
Bar 24b–25.	**A²**: RH slur over barline ends before bar 25 RH chord 1, but its curve indicates continuation to this chord (cf. also RH slur bar 32a RH note 4 to bar 25 RH chord 1)
Bar 26.	**A²**: lack of ✲ on beat 3 may suggest open pedal until end of work
Bar 27.	Slur to RH notes 1–3 from **A¹** and by analogy with bar 26
Bars 28, 31.	Slur to RH notes 1–3 by analogy with bar 26
Bars 31–32a/b.	RH slur over barline by analogy with **A¹** bars 39–40
Bars 32b–33, 33–34, 48a–33.	RH slurs over barline by analogy with bars 34–35
Bar 36.	LH beat 1: crotchet rest from **A¹**.
Bars 47–48a.	RH slur over barline from **A¹**, **C**

WALTZ in A♭ major (composed 1835)

Sources

A¹	Autograph, dedicated and dated 'pour Mlle Marie, Drezno Sept. 1835' (now lost). Reproduced in Leopold Binental, *Chopin / W 120-tą rocznicę urodzin / Dokumenty i pamiątki* (Warsaw: Łazarski, 1930).
A²	Autograph, dedicated and dated 'à Mme Peruzzi hommage de Chopin 1837'. [US-Wdrl]
A³	Autograph, dedicated and dated 'à Mademoiselle Charlotte de Rothschild, hommage F. Chopin, Paris 1842'. [F-Pn: Ms. 121]
C¹	Copy, prepared by August Franchomme, dated 22 May 1850, presented to Jane Stirling. [Pl-Kj]
C²	Copy, prepared by August Franchomme, presented to his daughter Cécile. [F-Pn: Ms 10511]
C³	Copy, prepared by August Franchomme, carrying inscription 'à ma chère Juliette'. [France, private collection]
C⁴	Copy, prepared by unidentified copyist, based on same source as **C¹⁻³**. [F-Pn: D 10808]
C⁵	Copy, dated 1842, made for Mlle Marie Lichtenstein,

	attributed to Ferdinand da Costa. [D-LEdb]
F	French first edition, July 1855. J. Meissonnier Fils, Paris, plate no. J.M. 3526 (version by J. Fontana).
G	German first edition, July 1855. A. M. Schlesinger, Berlin, plate no. S. 4395 (version by J. Fontana).

Suggested filiation

There was a significant time lapse between the three autographs (1835–42). **C**[1,3,4] differ considerably from the other known sources; it is probable that these were based on a manuscript, now lost, which constituted a first draft of the composition. **C**[2] originally reproduced the text of the same unknown source, but its text was subsequently corrected to that of **A**[3]. The text of **C**[5] is close to that of **A**[2,3] but contains two unique variants.

Two versions are given here. The first is based on **A**[1], the most complete source. The second is based on **A**[3] and includes variants from **A**[2] and significant variants from **C**[5], **F** and **G**. The variants in **C**[1–4] are of greater musicological than practical interest and do not appear in the music text or Critical Commentary.

Version based on A[1]

Bars 8, 32.	Pedalling from **A**[2]
Bar 14.	The *stretto* should be understood as an expressive intensification rather than as an accelerando.
Bar 18.	Staccato dot to RH note 1 as in bar 20
Bars 18, 20, 21, 22.	**A**[1]: no augmentation dots to LH dotted minims; here as in **A**[3] (bars 18, 22), **C**[5] (bar 20), **A**[2] (bar 21)
Bars 25–40.	**A**[1]: indicated as repeat of bars 1–16
Bars 40, 48.	**A**[1] lacks right-facing repeat sign in bar 40 and corresponding left-facing repeat sign in bar 48 (dots to double barline are absent) - almost certainly an oversight; here as in **A**[2]
Bars 41, 43 *et seq.*	RH beat 1: crotchet rest from **A**[3]
Bars 43–44, 45–46, 47–48, 57–62, 63–64.	RH upper slur over barline from **A**[2, 3] and by analogy with bars 41–42, 42–43
Bar 45.	Accent to RH beat 2 from **A**[2] and by analogy with bars 61
Bar 48.	Slur to LH beats 1–2 as in bar 64. **A**[1]: slur from RH beat 3, which is not continued onto second leaf of autograph
Bars 58, 60, 62.	RH chords 2, 3: staccato dot from **A**[2, 3] and by analogy with bars 42, 44, 46
Bar 63.	Slur to LH chords 2, 3 from **A**[2] and by analogy with bars 47
Bar 64.	**A**[1] has left-facing repeat sign, but bar 48 lacks corresponding right-facing repeat sign (dots to double barline are absent). The decision to repeat or not to repeat bars 48–64 depends on one's view of whether the right-facing repeat sign was accidentally omitted in bar 48 (in which case repetition would ensue) or whether the left-facing repeat sign at bar 64 is redundant (no repeat required). A version without repetition of bars 48–64 appears in **A**[2].

Version based on A[3] with variants

Unless indicated otherwise, all indications within parentheses are from **A**[2]. LH minims in **C**[5] are systematically notated without augmentation dot except in bars 20 and 22.

Bars 1, 3, 4, 5.	**A**[2]: no augmentation dot to LH note 1
Bars 6, 30.	Pedalling from **A**[1]
Bar 7.	**C**[5]: no ♮ to RH note 4
Bars 11, 35.	Variant from **A**[2]: notes 1–13 quavers, not semiquavers; second variant (in footnote) from **G**, **F**: notes 1–12 quavers, not semiquavers
Bar 16.	*Fine* from **A**[1] (see comment to bar 64). **A**[2]: RH note 3 spelt cb^2, not $b\natural^1$. Left-facing repeat sign from **A**[2].
Bars 17–23.	**A**[3]: bars 17–23 repeated in full, but following details are omitted: augmentation dot to LH dotted minims bars 17, 20, 22 chord 1; LH arpeggio sign bar 19 chord 1; LH slurs bars 19–22; RH slur bars 23–24b (here by analogy with bars 23–24a). **C**[5]: repeat of bars 17–23 also indicated by repeat sign (right-facing sign wrongly placed after bar 16 beat 2, left-facing at bar 24a).
Bars 18, 20, 22.	**C**[5]: accent notated as '∧' above RH note 5
Bars 19, 23b.	LH crotchet rests added to clarify counterpoint and by analogy with similar bars
Bar 20.	**A**[3]: no augmentation dot to LH dotted minims; here as in **C**[5]. **A**[2] LH chord 1: eb, g notated as crotchets.
Bar 21.	**A**[3]: no augmentation dots to LH dotted minims; here as in **A**[2]
Bars 21, 22.	**A**[2] has two separate slurs in upper LH voice (i.e. LH notes 1–3)
Bar 24a.	Slur to LH beats 2, 3 from **A**[1]
Bar 24b.	Crotchet rest to LH beat 1 from **A**[1]
Bars 25–40.	**A**[2,3]: indicated as repeat of bar 1 to bar 16 beat 2
Bar 41.	**A**[2]: repeat sign at start of this bar, not after bar 40 beat 2; consequently bar 48a ends with current RH chord 2 of bar 40 (see footnote variant on p. 87)
Bars 41–42 *et seq.*	**A**[2]: slur (situated above RH) from RH beat 2 bar 42 to RH beat 1 bar 43; in consequence, no slur under lower RH voice
Bars 43–44, 47–48, 59–60, 63–64.	Slur under lower RH voice from **A**[1]
Bar 55.	Dynamic progression suggests continuation of broken *crescendo* line to the climax
Bar 56.	RH ⌢ from **A**[1], **C**[5]; LH ⌢ from **C**[5]
Bars 56–64.	**A**[2,3], **C**[5]: indicated as repeat of earlier bars. In **A**[3], Chopin puts 'Trio da capo' after bar 56 beat 2, indicating repetition of entire Trio (see also **C**[5]). By contrast, at corresponding place in **A**[2], he writes 'Trio da capo al fine', denoting reprise of first section only of Trio (for location of 'fine' see footnote variant on p. 87). It is thus possible to omit the repetition of bars 49–64 in performance.
Bar 64.	**A**[2,3], **C**[5]: reprise of first part of waltz could not be indicated here for reasons outlined in comment to bars 56–64; here as in **A**[1], **C**[1–4]

WALTZ in F minor (composed 1842)

Sources

A[1]	Autograph, dedicated and dated 'à Mademoiselle Marie de Krudner, Paris, le 8 déc. 1842'. [F-Pn: W.20 (1)]
A[2]	Autograph, dedicated and dated 'à Madame Oury, Paris 10 Décembre 1842'. [US: private collection]
A[3]	Autograph, dedicated 'à Mlle Elise Gavard'. [F-Pn: Ms. 117]
A[4]	Autograph, dedicated 'à Mme la C[sse] Eszterhazy'. [France, Abbaye de Royaumont (F. Lang's collection)]
A[5]	Autograph, bequeathed by the Rothschild family. [F-Pn: Ms 110]

C¹	Copy, prepared by unidentified copyist, based on **A³**. [F-Po: Rés. 50 (3)]
C²	Copy, prepared by unidentified copyist, based on **A⁴**, formerly owned by Franchomme family. [F-Pn: D. 11768]
C³	Copy, attributed to Princess Marcelina Czartoryska, based on **A³** but containing inaccuracies. [private collection, owner unknown]
C⁴	Incomplete copy, prepared by Julian Fontana, based on **P**. [PL-B: Rps 650 II]
P	Polish first edition, 1852. I. Wildt, Cracow, plate no. 3, based on autograph in album of Countess Plater (now lost).
E¹	English first edition, July 1853. Wessel & Co., London, plate no. W & Cº Nº 8015.
E²	English second edition, April 1854. J. J. Ewer, London, without plate no.
F	French first edition, July 1855. J. Meissonnier Fils, Paris, plate no. J.M. 3527 (version by J. Fontana).
G	German first edition, July 1855. A. M. Schlesinger, Berlin, plate no. S. 4396 (version by J. Fontana).

Because of the richness of sources three different versions are given. The first reproduces the text of **A³**. The second is based on **A⁵** and includes variant readings from **A¹,²,⁴**. The third is based on **P**, which itself was based on an autograph from 1844 (now lost), in all probability Chopin's last manuscript of this work.

Version based on A³

Bar 1.	RH note 1 requires fresh attack in reprise
Bars 1, 2, 10, 11, 37.	LH crotchet rest from **P**
Bar 3.	Crotchet rest LH beat 3 added to clarify counterpoint
Bar 18.	**A³** RH note 3: no ♮
Bar 20b.	After beat 2, Chopin gives right-facing repeat sign indicating repeat of bars 21–52, but without specifying corresponding left-facing repeat sign at bar 52; here no repeat signs as in **A¹,²,⁴,⁵**
Bars 22, 38.	RH notes 1–4: this unusual notation of Chopin's amounts to a transcribed mordant on the beat - a subtle variant of the triplet in bars 30, 46. **A³**: no tie to RH notes 3–4.
Bar 27.	**A³** RH chord 2: no ♮ to bb^1
Bars 36–37.	**A³**: RH slur over barline ends after bar 36, although continuation to bar 37 (on new system) clearly intended; here as in **A⁴,⁵** bars 36–38
Bar 37.	**A³**: LH omitted; here as in **A¹**
Bars 38–46.	Notated in **A³** as exact repetition of bars 22–30, though with variant of LH part in final bar (i.e. bar 46)

Version based on A⁵ with variants

Slurs of different length from **A⁵** and **A¹,²,⁴** are discussed in the Critical Commentary do not appear in the music text itself. Crotchet rests within parentheses are from **P**.

Bar 1.	*Allegretto* from **A¹**; *legato* from **A⁴**
Bars 1–4.	**A¹,²**: slur over barlines breaks at bar 2 RH note 3, new slur begins bar 3 RH note 1; identical slurring in **A⁴** except end of slur uncertain in bar 2
Bar 3.	LH beat 3: crotchet rest added to clarify counterpoint
Bars 5–12.	**A¹,²**: one continuous slur from RH note 1 bar 5 to RH note 3 bar 10; then slur from bar 11 RH note 1 to bar 12 RH note 3. **A⁴**: one continuous slur ending RH note 3 bar 12.
Bar 18.	**A⁴,⁵**: no ♮ to RH note 3. **A¹**: slur ends RH note 6 (no slurring in bars 19–20a). **A¹,²**: $f\sharp^1$, not gb^1, to LH chord 3.
Bar 19.	**A²**: slur ends RH note 6 (no slurring in bar 20a)
Bar 20a.	⎯⎯⎯ from **A⁴**. **A⁵**: minim on RH beat 1 is not original (added in pencil to clarify counterpoint); no double barline or right-facing repeat sign. **A⁴**: slur ends RH note 1, then another slur for RH notes 2–7.
Bar 20b.	**A¹**: slur begins RH note 2
Bars 21–22.	**A⁵**: ambiguous slur apparently from bar 21 RH note 3 to bar 23 RH note 2; here as in **A²,⁴**
Bars 25–27.	**A¹,²**: single slur bars 25–26; another begins from bar 27 RH note 1
Bars 25–30.	**A⁴**: separate slur for each of bars 25, 26, then one continuous slur for bars 27–30
Bar 28.	RH slur ends RH chord 1 in **A¹,²**; new slur begins RH note 2 in **A²**
Bars 34–35.	**A²**: slur ends bar 34 RH chord 2; single slur for bar 35
Bars 35–38.	**A¹**: slur ends bar 35 RH chord 1; no slurring in bars 36–38
Bar 36.	**A²,⁵**: semiquaver rest, not dotted quaver rest, to RH beat 2
Bars 41–43.	**A¹,²**: same slurring as in bars 25–27
Bars 41–44.	**A⁴**: single slur from bar 41 RH note 1 to bar 44 RH chord 1
Bar 44.	**A²**: slurring here as in bar 28. **A¹**: slur ends RH note 2
Bar 52.	Because of upbeat at beginning of piece, this bar has only two beats in **A¹,²**; although one would expect **A⁴** to be similar, Chopin gives augmentation dot to RH minim and rest on LH beat 3. **A⁵**: no LH rest.

Version based on P

Bar 20a.	**P**: augmentation dot to minim RH note 1. Here no augmentation dot to eliminate semitone clash between RH eb^1 and LH $e\natural^1$ beat 3 (cf. version based on **A³**); consequently, editorial crotchet rest has been added. Arpeggio sign to LH beat 3 facilitates playing of this chord.
Bars 27, 43.	♮ to b^1 in RH chord 4 from **A¹,²,⁴,⁵** (obvious omission in **P**)
Bar 34.	LH chords 2, 3 also contain eb^1, manifestly an engraving error
Bar 45.	Augmentation dot to LH minim omitted; here as in **A¹,³,⁴**

WALTZ in A minor (composed 1847)

Sources

A¹	Autograph. [F-Pn: Ms. 119A]
A²	Autograph. [F-Pn: Ms. 119B]

The principal source for this edition is **A²**, the later of the two autographs.

Bars 5, 29.	**A¹** LH note 1: *A*, not *a*
Bar 8.	**A¹** LH chord 2: $g–c^1–e^1$
Bars 9, 10.	**A¹**: dotted rhythm on RH beat 1 is more appropriate to mazurka than waltz
Bar 15.	*tr* above RH note 1 from **A¹**
Bar 16.	**A¹**: crotchet rest on LH beat 3
Bars 17–24, 25–40.	**A¹**: no repeat signs for these passages

Bars 18, 19, 20, 22, 23.
A¹: ∾, not grace notes, to RH beat 1
Bar 24. **A¹** LH note chords 2, 3: *a–c¹–e¹*, not *e–a–c¹*
Bars 27, 39. **A²**: no ♭ to LH chord 3; here as in **A¹**
Bar 32. **A¹**: additional *e¹* in LH chord 2
Bar 39. **A¹**: single grace note *f♯²* on RH beat 1
Bars 43–44. **A²**: RH slur ends RH note 3; here as in bars 27–28
Bars 47–56. No LH part in **A¹**
Bars 55–56. **A²**: RH slur seems to end before barline; here by analogy with bars 39–40

APPENDIX

WALTZ OP. 18 (Version based on **A¹**)

A¹ presents the musical text in a highly condensed form, and includes a number of repeats using first-, second- and third-time bars and reprise indications typical of Chopin's notational practice. Bars 29–35, 61–66, 69–98, 133–148, notated in **A¹** by such means, are reproduced in their entirety here.

Bars 5–6. **A¹**: slurs to bar 5 RH notes 2–3, bar 5 RH note 4 to bar 6 RH note 1; here as in bars 13–14
Bar 13. Staccato dot to RH note 1 from **A²,³**
Bars 43, 75. LH crotchet rest from **A²,³**
Bars 46, 48 *et seq*.
Staccato dot to RH notes 2, 3 from **A²,³**
Bars 51–51b. RH slur over barline by analogy with bars 51–51a
Bars 57, 65, 89, 97.
A¹: ♮ added in pencil to *g♭¹* RH chord 2 (not in Chopin's hand). Accent to RH note 3 possibly redundant.
Bars 58, 90, 98.
A¹ RH note 1: no ♮
Bars 59, 91, 99.
A¹ LH chord 2: no ♮ to *g♭*
Bar 67. **A¹** RH note 1: ∾, not ∾
Bars 117–119, 125–127, 156.
LH crotchet rest added to clarify counterpoint
Bars 127–132.
A¹: incorrect LH key signature (six ♭s, not five)
Bars 149–156b.
A¹: incorrect LH key signature (five ♭s, not six)
Bar 159. > to RH note 1 by analogy with bars 157, 158

WALTZ OP. 18 (Version based on **A²**)

Bar 28a. RH slur from **A³** and by analogy with bar 52
Bar 29. Staccato dot to RH note 1 by analogy with bar 5
Bar 67. Augmentation dot to LH note 1 from **A¹,³** and by analogy with bar 99
Bars 73, 105. **A²**: RH chord 4 has downward stem only; upward stem to *g♭²* here by analogy with bars 74, 106
Bar 75. RH chord 4: *e♭²*, *g♭¹* share downward stem; here as in **A³** and by analogy with bar 107
Bars 77, 81, 85, 88.
A² RH chord 2: no ♮ to *g♭¹*
Bars 78, 82, 86, 89.
A² RH note 1: no ♮ to *g♭¹*
Bar 80 Upward stem to LH chord 4 as in bar 88
Bars 80, 88. **A²**: no ♮ to *d♭* LH chord 2, *d♭²* RH note 3
Bar 83. **A²** LH chord 2: no ♮ to *g♭*
Bar 86. **A²**: staccato dot to RH note 3; here staccato wedge as in **A³**

Bar 89. RH staccato dots by analogy with bar 90
Bars 99–100. LH slur over barline as in bars 67–68
Bars 120, 170.
Optional ♮ to *d♭¹* in LH chord 2 by analogy with bar 112
Bars 123–124b.
RH slur by analogy with bars 123–124a
Bar 129. **A²**: no ♮ to RH note 2
Bars 130, 138.
A² LH chord 2: no ♮ to *a♭*
Bar 135. RH slur from **A³** and by analogy with bar 127
Bar 140. **A²**: no ♮ to RH note 4
Bar 155. Staccato dot to RH note 2 from **A³**
Bars 155–156a.
Slur over barline from **A³**
Bars 155–156b.
Slur over barline by analogy with bars 155–156a
Bar 157. **A²**: incorrect LH key signature (five ♭s, not six)
Bar 171. **A²**: no ♮ to RH note 4
Bar 175. Staccato dot to RH note 1 from **A³**
Bar 178. **A²** LH chord 1: no ♮ to *g♭*
Bar 179. **A²** RH chord 1: no ♮ to *d♭¹*

WALTZ OP. 34 NO. 1 (Version based on **A¹**)

Bar 7. **A¹**: according to commentary accompanying the reconstruction published in *Kwartalnik muzyczny*, Chopin first notated, then deleted, *E♭* LH note 1; however this note does appear, though very faintly, in a published facsimile
Bars 11, 12. LH slur by analogy with RH slurring
Bars 12, 34, 36, 58, 60.
A¹: accent in RH, owing to lack of space; here *dim.* hairpin by analogy with bars 2, 40b (see also bars 6, 10, 11)
Bar 17. **A¹**: 𝄋 appears at beginning of bar because of compressed notation (see comment to bars 41–62); 𝄋 moved here to bar 41, as bars 17–40b should certainly not be repeated during the *da capo*
Bars 30, 54. Arpeggio sign by analogy with bar 26
Bars 37, 38, 39, 61, 62, 63.
A¹: no hairpins to RH; here by analogy with bars 33 and 40b
Bars 38, 62. **A¹**: no LH long accents; here by analogy with bar 37
Bars 39a–40a, 63a–64a.
RH slur from **A²**
Bars 39b–40b.
RH slurs by analogy with bars 33–34
Bar 39b. **A¹**: illegible accidental to RH note 6 (♭ possible)
Bars 41–62. **A¹**: indicated as repeat of bars 17–38. Bars 63b–64b have indication '3ᵐᵉ volta'. Thus it is difficult to know whether or not bars 57–62 should be repeated. Here they are repeated as in **A²**.
Bar 63b. **A¹**: no augmentation dot to LH minim; here as in bar 39a
Bars 78–80. Pedalling from **F**, **G**, **E**
Bar 82. **A¹**: RH notes 4–7 mistakenly notated as demisemiquavers
Bar 83. **A¹**: no ♭ to RH note 10
Bar 86. **A¹**: RH notes 2–9 mistakenly notated as demisemiquavers
Bar 87. **A¹**: no ♭ to RH note 10, no ♮ to RH note 13
Bar 93. **A¹**: no RH slur; here as in bar 77

Bars 98, 130. Pedal as in bar 97

Bars 98, 105, 106, 130, 137, 138.
  A¹ RH beat 1: no ♭ to g^1

Bars 101–102, 133–134.
  Pedalling from **A²** (bars 133–134), which is more suited to modern piano

Bars 108, 111, 140, 143. ❀ from **F**, **G**, **E**

Bar 112b. Upward stem to RH note 2 indicates that it belongs equally to the melody

Bar 123. **A¹**: LH note 1 notated as F♭ (although ♭ is almost illegible); here E♮ in accordance with harmonic context (see also **A²** bars 125, 127)

Bars 129–143. Indicated as repeat of bars 97–111

Bars 143–144. Slur over barline from **A²**

Bars 154, 157, 158.
  A¹ RH chord 1: augmentation dot(s) missing

Bar 160. **A¹**: ❀ lacks corresponding 𝄢𝄡.

Bars 162–164. **A¹**: no ♭s to RH / LH Gs

Bar 164. **A¹**: no ♮

Bar 166. RH note 1: accent suggested by musical context

Bar 167. **A¹**: illegible feature crossed out before RH dotted minim; here grace note as in similar bars. No ♭ to RH note 10.

Bar 173. **A¹** LH chord 2: no eb^1; here as in bar 157

Bars 173–175. RH slurs over barline by analogy with bars 77–79

Bar 174. **A¹**: no ♭ to g^1 RH chord 4

Bars 175–176. Pedalling from **F**, **G**, **E**

Bar 176. **A¹** LH chord 1: Db_1 notated with '8'

WALTZ OP. 64 NO. 1
(Version based on **A³** with variants)

Bar 20. LH crotchet rest as in bars 21–23

Bars 20, 32. **A³**: ♮ to RH note 4 accidentally omitted

Bar 21. **A**^{3,5} LH chord 2: no ♭ to eb^1

Bars 21–23. LH crotchet rest from **A⁵**

Bar 24. **A**^{3,5}: ♮ to RH note 4 accidentally omitted

Bar 32. **A**$^{3-5}$: ♮ to RH note 4 accidentally omitted

Bar 36b. No slur ending on RH note 1 in any source; here by analogy with bars 35–36a

Bars 41–48. **A⁴**: one continuous RH slur

Bars 43–44. **A⁵**: RH slur ends at end of bar 43; single RH slur to bar 44

Bars 45–48. **A⁵**: RH slur begins bar 45 RH note 1

Bar 50. No ♮ to gb LH chord 2 in any source. **A³**: no ♮ to RH note 3.

Bar 51. ❀ from **A⁶**

Bars 53–72. **A⁵**: no slurring except to bars 53–63 RH notes 1–2

Bars 56–63. Slurs to RH notes 1, 2 from **A**^{4,5}

Bars 56–68. **A⁴**: RH slurring as follows:

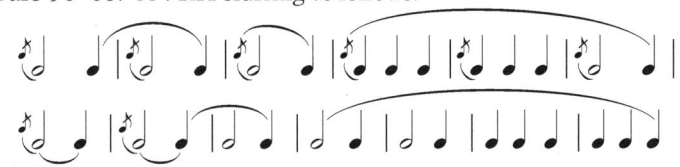

Bar 66. RH slur by analogy with bar 65

Bars 69–72. **A³**: each dotted minim marked with *tr*, followed by wavy line which curls upwards (indicating separate trills); here one long wavy line as in **A**^{4,5}. **A⁵**: dotted minims not tied.

Bar 73. **A⁴**: RH slur begins RH note 1

WALTZ OP. 64 NO. 2 (Version based on **A²**)

Bar 9. RH slur from **A³** and by analogy with bar 25

Bars 11, 27. RH slur by analogy with bars 25, 29

Bar 16. **A²**: no LH rest

Bars 21–22. RH slur over barline from **A³** and by analogy with bars 5–6

Bar 26. **A²**: ♯ to RH note 2, marked in pencil (not in Chopin's hand)

Bar 45. **A²**: ♮ to $d\#^1$ in LH chord 2, marked in pencil (not in Chopin's hand)

Bars 49–64. **A²**: indicated as repeat of bars 33–48

Bars 89–91. **A²**: RH slur over barlines ends bar 90 RH note 3; here as in bars 73–75

Bars 91–96. **A²**: RH slur over barlines begins bar 92 RH note 1; here by analogy with bars 75–80

Bar 94. **A²** LH chord 2: no ♮ to gb^1

Bar 97. RH slur from **A³** and by analogy with bar 33

Bars 98–128. **A²**: indicated as repeat of bars 34–48 (beats 1, 2). Crotchet rests on beat 3 of the final bar (bar 128) are editorial.